GAMBLING — WHO WINS?

CHAPTER I	**Gambling — An American Tradition**	2
	The Reform Movement ... The Wild, Wild West ... The Progressive Era — A Second Period of Reform ... Legal Gambling Becomes Acceptable Again ... Gamblers Anonymous	
CHAPTER II	**An Overview of Gambling**	5
	Some Definitions ... Types of Gambling ... A Very Big Business ... Gross Wagers (The Handle) ... Gross Revenues ... The Take-out ... How Much Does the House Keep? ... Illegal Gambling ... Gambling on Indian Reservations	
CHAPTER III	**Pari-Mutuel Betting — Horses, Dogs, and Jai-Alai**	12
	How Pari-Mutuel Betting Works ... How Old Do You Have to Be to Gamble? ... Horse Racing ... Dog Racing ... Jai-Alai ... Off-Track Betting (OTB)	
CHAPTER IV	**Casino Gambling**	20
	First, Casinos in Nevada ... And Then New Jersey ... Now Casinos Are Almost Everywhere ... Casino Games ... Casino Revenues ... Casino Gambling Spreads Across the Country ... A Growing Business	
CHAPTER V	**Lotteries**	28
	A Part of American History ... New Lotteries Begin ... Types of Lottery Games ... Lottery Sales ... Lottery Prizes ... How Much Does the Government Get in Taxes ... Lotteries — The Whole World Plays	
CHAPTER VI	**Public Opinion About Gambling**	34
	How Americans Gamble ... Does Gambling Cause Trouble? The Council on Compulsive Gambling Survey ... Attitudes About Gambling ... Why Do People Gamble?	
CHAPTER VII	**The Debate Over the Lottery**	41
	The Lottery is a Good Idea ... The Lottery is a Bad Idea	
GLOSSARY		49
IMPORTANT NAMES AND ADDRESSES		50
RESOURCES		51
INDEX		52

INFORMATION PLUS
WYLIE, TEXAS 75098
© 1992, 1995
ALL RIGHTS RESERVED

EDITORS:
NORMA JONES, B.A.
NANCY R. JACOBS, M.A.
MARK A. SIEGEL, Ph.D.

CHAPTER I

GAMBLING — AN AMERICAN TRADITION

Gambling was very popular in North America, even before there was a United States. By the end of the 1600s, just about every large city in colonial America (English colonies before the American Revolution in 1776) had a large lottery wheel. Playing with cards or dice was very common. George Washington liked to play cards, and Benjamin Franklin printed and sold playing cards. The British Stamp Act, which helped cause the American Revolution, put a one-shilling tax on playing cards. This angered the colonists as much as the tax on tea. In the South, betting on horse racing was very popular.

During the colonial period, lotteries were a very popular way to raise money. In England, a lottery was used to raise money to establish the colony of Virginia. The Virginia Company held a lottery to pay for a settlement at Jamestown, Virginia. In 1748, young Ben Franklin organized a lottery to pay for military supplies to defend the City of Philadelphia from attack by Indian and French soldiers.

In 1777, the Continental Congress held a $5 million lottery to pay for the Revolutionary War. Lotteries were also used to raise money to build bridges, help churches and schools, and to aid the needy. Lotteries were used to raise money to help found such famous schools as Harvard, Yale, Columbia, Princeton, and Dartmouth.

During the 1800s, Americans were known for their gambling. Visitors said it was impossible to talk with a Kentuckian without hearing the phrase, "I'll bet you!" President Andrew Jackson liked to gamble. He was followed by Martin Van Buren who bet a new suit and $40,000 that he would win his run for the presidency.

Large riverboats went up and down the Mississippi and Ohio Rivers carrying passengers or freight. Those that carried passengers almost always had a casino where gamblers played roulette, cards, and other forms of gambling with the passengers. At the end of the Mississippi River was the City of New Orleans, a city noted for gambling. Meanwhile, New York City had approximately 6,000 gambling houses in 1850, that is one gambling house for every 85 New Yorkers.

THE REFORM MOVEMENT

During the 1840s, a reforming spirit swept across the United States. Many societies formed to protest the use of tobacco, swearing, and even the moving of mail on Sunday. The first women's' rights movement was founded, and temperance crusaders preached against drinking alcohol. During these years, the abolitionist movement to get rid of slavery became stronger.

Many reformers attacked gambling because so many lotteries were run by people who stole the money and left town. Reformers also felt that many people who bought lottery tickets could not afford them and bought them instead of taking care of their families. As a result of these reform efforts, most states began to outlaw lotteries. By 1860, every state in the nation except Delaware, Kentucky, and Missouri had passed laws making lotteries and many other forms of gambling illegal.

That did not mean that gambling disappeared. Gambling took place openly in such cities as New York, Chicago, and New Orleans. The police were often paid (bribed) to look the other way while illegal gambling continued. For some people, the fact that gambling was illegal made it more exciting.

THE WILD, WILD WEST

The opening of the far western part of the country during the mid-1880s gave gambling in America a second life. Far from both government controls and the Eastern reformers who wanted to outlaw gambling, the West became a center for gambling. Every town located near a mining camp, a railroad, or a major cattle trail had a gambling hall. Major gambling houses could easily be found in Kansas City, Dallas, Denver, and San Francisco.

THE PROGRESSIVE ERA — A SECOND PERIOD OF REFORM

Between 1900 and 1917, a reform-minded group of people called the "Progressives" worked very hard to stop corruption and dishonest behavior in business and government. They helped improve working and living conditions for women, children, and the poor. They also attacked things they considered morally wrong, such as drinking and gambling. As a result, most states outlawed gambling.

By the 1920s, organized crime took over illegal gambling. Illegal gamblers were even able to fix the 1919 World Series. In this "Black Sox" Scandal, the Chicago White Sox deliberately lost the series to the Cincinnati Reds to guarantee that the gamblers would win. Organized crime controlled all types of gambling from betting on horses, to wagering on sporting events, to betting on numbers. The federal government sometimes tried to stop this illegal gambling but could never eliminate it.

LEGAL GAMBLING AGAIN BECOMES ACCEPTABLE

Since 1970, the United States has changed its attitude towards gambling. Three hundred years ago, gambling, especially lotteries, was seen as a proper way for government to raise money. Over the past several years, slow economic growth, cuts in federal aid to state and city governments, and growing public needs have forced many desperate state and local governments to look for new ways to get more money. As a result, most states have turned to lotteries and horse and dog racing to try to raise more funds.

Politicians do not like to raise taxes because they want the people to like them and keep electing them to office. Several states have turned to casino gambling as a way to "painlessly" gain money for the government. Native-American reservations have also turned to gambling in order to raise money. Fewer Americans now see gambling as something bad that might cause people to lose money they need or might attract organized crime. Instead, more and more Americans are seeing it as an opportunity to raise money for government so that taxes will not have to be raised. Furthermore, if people want to gamble, say some supporters of gambling, the government has no right to stop them.

GAMBLERS ANONYMOUS

For most people who bet, gambling is a form of recreation and fun. For some people, however, gambling is a compulsion, a disease they cannot control. These people may become addicted to gambling (like some people become addicted to alcohol or drugs) and it may take control of their behavior. Like alcoholism, the addiction may destroy their lives. Gamblers Anonymous offers a 12-step program similar to Alcoholics Anonymous.

Currently, an estimated 12,000 people go to Gamblers Anonymous meetings at about 800 locations across the nation. All members share two goals — to stop themselves from gambling and to help other compulsive gamblers to do the same. Gamblers Anonymous can be reached by calling (213) 386-8789 or writing Gamblers Anonymous, International Service Office, P.O. Box 17173, Los Angeles, CA 90017. The organization will supply anyone who requests with the location of the nearest Gamblers Anonymous. All information is kept confidential — no one else will know.

CHAPTER II

AN OVERVIEW OF GAMBLING

SOME DEFINITIONS

Like any subject, gambling has its own special vocabulary. In order to understand what goes on in gambling, certain terms must be understood. The following words are some that people who work in the gambling business use.

- GAMING — the act or practice of gambling; putting certain amounts of money at risk with the hope of winning more.

- WAGER — means the same as "bet," the amount of money a person spends or "puts down" on a gambling activity. For example: *The bettor wagered $10 on the horse race.*

- HANDLE — the total amount of money bet by all bettors on some form or game of chance. The daily handle at a horse race track is the total amount of money people bet on the horses that day at the track.

- TAKE-OUT — the percentage or amount of the handle that is taken out by the person or company that operates the gambling activity (the race track owner, for example), and the state government, mostly in the form of taxes. The racetrack owner uses his or her part of the take-out to pay the winning horse, to operate the track, and to make a profit.

- PAY-OFF — the amount of money gotten from the bets which is left after the take-out. This amount is then given back to the winning bettors.

TYPES OF LEGAL GAMBLING

There are five main types of legal gambling in the United States — bingo, lotteries, pari-mutuel betting, off-track betting, and casinos. Legal gambling can be operated by either a state or private enterprise or business. While there are some federal laws which control gambling, most gambling is controlled by state laws.

In 1993, some form of gambling was permitted in 49 states plus Washington, DC, Puerto Rico, and the U.S. Virgin Islands. Hawaii was the only state that did not permit gambling. Bingo is, by far, the most common form of legal gambling (47 states, Washington, DC, and Puerto Rico). Most states have some form of lottery and/or horse racing. Table 2.1 shows what types of gambling are permitted in which states and territories. Table 2.2 gives the same information for the provinces and territories in Canada.

A VERY BIG BUSINESS

Gambling is a very big business. In 1993, legal gambling companies earned $34.7 billion (earnings come from gamblers' losses). Americans spent more money on gambling in 1993 than they did going to the movies, attending sports events, going to live concerts, taking trips on cruise ships, playing video games, and buying flowers and plants (Figure 2.1). In fact, Americans lost six times more money gambling than they spent on going to the movies.

If the total $34.7 billion lost by gam-

TABLE 2.1
U.S. gaming at a glance

	B	Ch	CR	Cs	D	S	V	K	I	L	N	P	G	J	H	Q	T	S	I	O	P
Alabama	•	•											•		♠	•	•	•			
Alaska	•	•																			
Arizona	•	•		•	•			•	•				•			•	•	•	•	•	
Arkansas													•		♠	•	•				
California	•	•	•					•	•	•	•	□			•	•	•	•	•	•	
Colorado	•	•	•	•	•			•	•	•		□	•			•	•	•	•	•	
Connecticut	•	•		•	•			•	•	•	•	□	•	•	♠	♠	♠	•	•	•	•
Delaware	•	•				□	♠		•	•	•	□			•		•	•			
Florida	•	•							•	•	•		•	•	•	•	•	•	•		
Georgia	•								★	★	★										
Hawaii																					
Idaho	•	★		★					•	•			•			•	•	•	•		
Illinois	•	•	♠	•	•			□	•	•	•	□			•	•	•	•	•	•	
Indiana	•	•		♠	♠				•	•	•				♠	♠	♠	♠	♠	♠	
Iowa	•	•	•	•	•				•	•			•		•	•	•	•			
Kansas	•	•					•		•	•	•		•		□	•	•	•			
Kentucky	•	•							•	•	•				•	•	•	•	•	•	•
Louisiana	•	•		★	★				•	•	•			□	•	•	•	•	•		
Maine	•	•							•	•	•	□			•	□	•		★		
Maryland	•	•	•		•				•	•	•	□			•		•	•	•	•	♠
Massachusetts	•	•						★	•	•	•	□	•		•	□	•	★	★		
Michigan	•	•		•	•			•	•	•	•	•			•	•	•	•			
Minnesota	•	•	•	•	•				•	•	•				□	□	□	•	♠		
Mississippi	•	•		•	•																
Missouri	•	•		★	★				•	•	•				⊔	⊔	⊔	♠	♠		
Montana	•	•	•	•	•	•		•	•	•					♠	•	•	•	•		
Nebraska	•	•						•	★	★						•	•	•	•	★	
Nevada	•		•	•	•	•	•						□	□	□	•	•			•	•
New Hampshire	•	•							•	•	•	□	•		•		•	•	•		
New Jersey	•	•	★	•	•				•	•	•	□			•		•	•	•	★	
New Mexico	•	•		★	★										•	•	•	•			
New York	•	•		★					•	•	•	•	□		□	•	•	•	•	•	
North Carolina	•																				
North Dakota	•	•	•	•	•	•									•	•	•	•	♠	•	
Ohio	•	•							•	•	•	•			•	•	•	•	•	♠	
Oklahoma	•	•													♠	•	•	•	•		
Oregon	•	•	•	★	★	•		•	•	•	•	•	•			•	•	•	•		
Pennsylvania	•	•							•	•	•	•	□		•	□	•	•	•	•	•
Rhode Island	•	•						•	•	•	•	•	•	•	□		□	•			
South Carolina	•				•																
South Dakota	•	•					•		♠	•	•		□			•	•	•	•		
Tennessee															♠	♠	♠	♠	♠		
Texas	•	•							•	•	•		•			•	•	•			
Utah															■						
Vermont	•	•							•	•	•	□	□		•		□	♠			

(Continued on following page.)

6

blers was thought of as the sales of one single company, that company would have been the 12th largest company in the United States, ahead of Proctor and Gamble, the giant producer of laundry powder and other household products, slightly ahead of K Mart ($34.5 billion) and just behind the giant car maker, Chrysler Corporation ($43.6 billion).

TABLE 2.1 (Continued)
U.S. gaming at a glance

	B	Ch	CR	Cs	D	S	V	K	I	L	N	P	G	J	H	Q	T	S	I	O	P
Virginia	●	●							●	●	●				♠	♠	♠	♠	♠	♠	
Washington	●	●	●	●			●		●	●	●				□	●	●	●	●	●	
Wash D.C.	●	●							●	●	●										
West Virginia	●	●			●	●	●	●	●	●	□	●			♠	●	●	●	●		
Wisconsin	●	●		●	●				●	●	★		●		♠	♠	♠	●	♠		
Wyoming	●	●													♠	●	●	●	♠	●	
Puerto Rico	●			●	●					●	●						●	●		●	
Virgin Islands		●						★				●					●	●			

Legend:
● Legal and operative
★ Implemented since June 1993
♠ Authorized but not yet implemented
□ Permitted by law and previously operative

Column Headings:
B Charitable Bingo
Ch Charitable Games
CR Card Rooms
Cs Casinos
D Gaming Devices
S Sports Wagering
Lottery Sub-Headings:
V Video Lottery Terminals
K Keno

N Numbers
P Passives
Parimutuel Sub-Headings
G Greyhound
J Jai Alai
H Harness
Q Quarter Horse
T Thoroughbred
S Interstate Inter-Track Wagering
I Intrastate Inter-Track Wagering

Source: *International Gaming & Wagering Business*, September 5, 1994

GROSS WAGERS (THE HANDLE)

Americans spent more than $394 billion on legal gambling in 1993. (See Table 2.3.) Three out of four dollars (75 percent) were wagered at casinos, mostly in Las Vegas, Nevada, and Atlantic City, New Jersey. Most of the rest (8 percent) was bet on the lotteries. Between 1982 and 1993, the amount of money bet on legal gambling more than tripled from $125.8 billion to $394.3 billion, a 213 percent increase.

GROSS REVENUES (THE TAKE-OUT)

The gross revenues or the take-out (how much the owners of the gambling casinos, the race tracks, etc., made) was $34.7 billion in 1993, more than three times the $10.4 billion they earned in 1982. (See Table 2.4.)

Most of the money made from gambling has been earned through the lotteries (37 percent) and casinos (36 percent). (See Table 2.5.) The $12.8 billion made from lotteries went to the state governments that run the lotteries. In the United States, only governments, not private companies, can operate a lottery in which people have to pay to buy a ticket in order to win. Total betting on horses, dogs, and jai-alai brought in about one in seven dollars (14 percent), while charitable games (5 percent) and bingo (4 percent) brought in most of the rest.

HOW MUCH DOES THE HOUSE KEEP?

Of the $394 billion bet in 1993, the U.S. gambling industry kept $34.7 billion, or about 8.8 percent of the amount bet. That means that, on the average, for every dollar that a bettor wagered, the state or the casino owner kept almost 9 cents and returned 91 cents in the form of winnings to the bettors. Different forms of gambling kept different amounts. The table games (for example, roulette, craps, and blackjack) and slot machines in Las Vegas and Atlantic City kept less than 9 percent, while the lotteries took a much higher percentage (41 percent). Operators of bingo, charitable games (usually

TABLE 2.2

Canadian gaming at a glance

	B	Ch	CR	Cs	D	S	V	K	I	L	N	P	G	J	H	Q	T	S	I	O	P
Alberta	•	•		•	•	•		•	•	•	•	•	•		•	•	•	•	•	•	•
British Columbia	•	•		•	•		•	•	•	•	•	•			•	•	•	•	•	♠	•
Manitoba	•	•		•	•		•	•	•	•	•	•	•		•	•	•	•	•	•	•
New Brunswick	•					□	•	•	•	•	•	•			•	♠	♠	♠	•	•	♠
Newfoundland	•	•	•			□	•	•	•	•	•	•			□	♠	□	♠	♠		♠
Northwest Terr.	•	•	•		•		•	•	•	•	•	•			♠	♠	♠	♠	♠	♠	♠
Nova Scotia	•	•		♠	♠	□	•	•	•	•	•	•		•	□	♠	♠	♠	•	•	♠
Ontario	•	•		★	★	•		•	•	•	•	•		•	•	•	•	•	•	•	□
Prince Edward Isl.	•	•				□	•	•	•	•	•	•			•	♠	♠	♠	♠		♠
Quebec	•			★	★		★	•	•	•	•	•		•	♠	□	♠	•	•	★	♠
Saskatchewan		•		•	•	•		•	•	•	•	•		•	•	•	•	•	•	•	♠
Yukon Terr.	•			•	•		•	•	•	•	•				♠	♠	♠	♠	♠	♠	♠

Columns grouped: Lottery Games | Parimutuel Wagering

Legend:
- • Legal and operative
- ★ Implemented since June 1993
- ♠ Authorized but not yet implemented
- □ Permitted by law and previously operative
- ■ Operative but no parimutuel wagering

Column Headings:
- B Charitable Bingo
- Ch Charitable Games
- CR Card Rooms
- Cs Casinos
- D Gaming Devices
- S Sports Wagering

Lottery Sub-Headings:
- V Video Lottery Terminals
- K Keno
- I Instant (& Pull-Tab) Games
- L Lotto
- N Numbers
- P Passives

Parimutuel Sub-Headings:
- G Greyhound
- J Jai Alai
- H Harness
- Q Quarter Horse
- T Thoroughbred
- S Interprovince Inter-Track Wagering
- I Intraprovince Inter-Track Wagering
- O Off-Track Betting
- P Telephone Betting

Note: Casinos in Alberta and British Columbia operate for charitable purposes only.

Source: *International Gaming & Wagering Business*, September 5, 1994

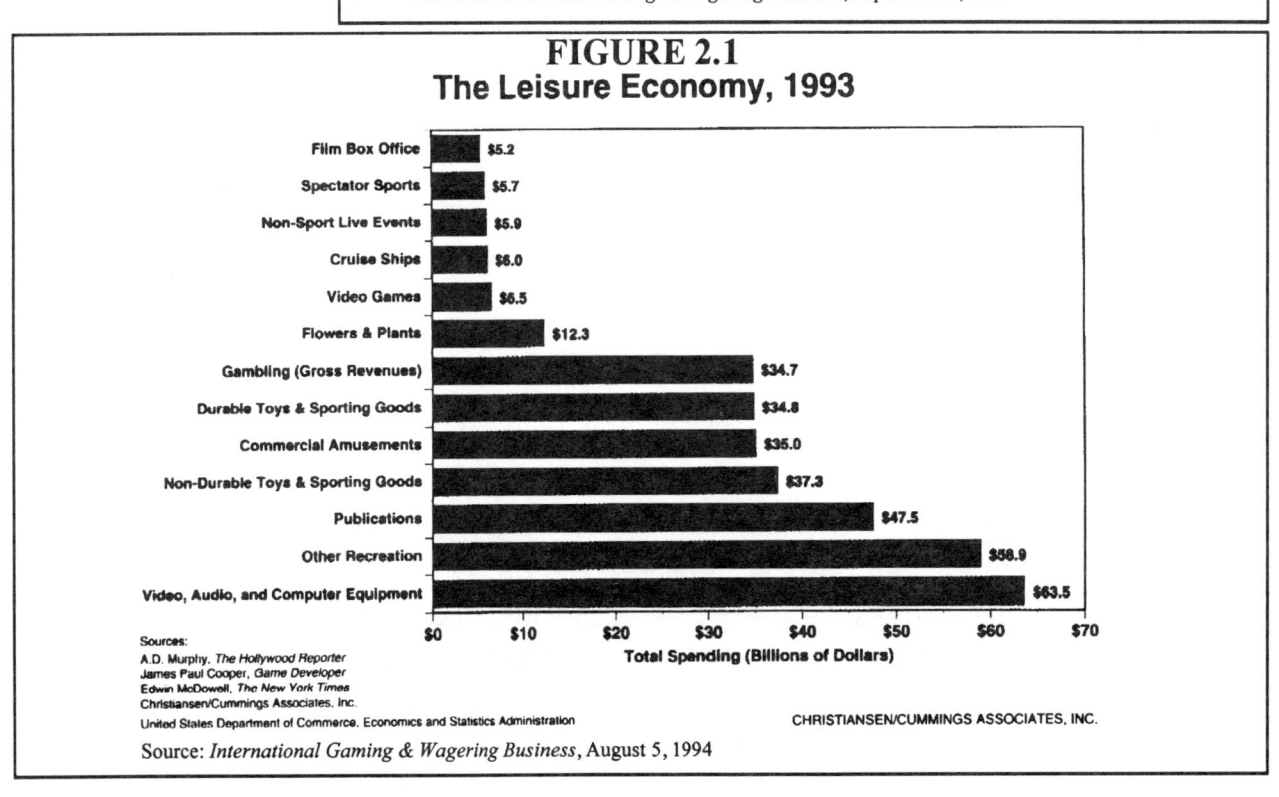

FIGURE 2.1
The Leisure Economy, 1993

Category	Total Spending (Billions of Dollars)
Film Box Office	$5.2
Spectator Sports	$5.7
Non-Sport Live Events	$5.9
Cruise Ships	$6.0
Video Games	$6.5
Flowers & Plants	$12.3
Gambling (Gross Revenues)	$34.7
Durable Toys & Sporting Goods	$34.8
Commercial Amusements	$35.0
Non-Durable Toys & Sporting Goods	$37.3
Publications	$47.5
Other Recreation	$58.9
Video, Audio, and Computer Equipment	$63.5

Sources:
A.D. Murphy, *The Hollywood Reporter*
James Paul Cooper, *Game Developer*
Edwin McDowell, *The New York Times*
Christiansen/Cummings Associates, Inc.
United States Department of Commerce, Economics and Statistics Administration

CHRISTIANSEN/CUMMINGS ASSOCIATES, INC.

Source: *International Gaming & Wagering Business*, August 5, 1994

casino type games), and gaming played on Indian Reservations kept more than one-fourth of the total amount bet.

ILLEGAL GAMBLING

Some Americans bet illegally. Most of these people bet on horse racing or sporting events such as football and basketball games. It is very hard to know how much is illegally bet every year. Because it is illegal, it is done secretly, and no public records are kept. *International Gaming & Wagering Business*, the monthly magazine which reports news of the gambling industry and gathers many statistics on gambling, has stopped estimating how much money is bet illegally. The editors of the magazine believe there is too little information on illegal gambling to make an estimate. In 1989, however, *International Gaming &*

TABLE 2.3

Trends in Gross Wagering, 1982 - 1993

(In $ millions)

	Gross Wagering (Handle) 1982	Gross Wagering (Handle) 1992 (Revised)	Gross Wagering (Handle) 1993	1982 - 1993 Gross Wagering Increase/(Decrease) Dollars	1982 - 1993 Percent	Average Annual Rate 1982-93
Pari-Mutuels						
Horses						
Tracks	$9,990.60	$9,381.80	$8,863.90	($1,126.70)	-11.28%	-1.08%
OTB	1,707.3	4,695.9	4,885.5	3,178.3	186.16%	10.03%
Total	11,697.9	14,077.7	13,749.4	2,051.5	17.54%	1.48%
Greyhounds						
Tracks	2,208.6	3,246.7	3,168.8	960.3	43.48%	3.34%
OTB		59.0	94.7	94.7	N/A	37.10% (1)
Total	2,208.6	3,305.7	3,263.5	1,054.9	47.76%	3.61%
Jai Alai	622.8	425.9	384.2	(238.6)	-38.32%	-4.30%
Total Pari-Mutuels	14,529.2	17,809.3	17,397.1	2,867.8	19.74%	1.65%
Lotteries						
Video Lotteries		2,450.3	3,878.3	3,878.3	N/A	N/A
Other Games	4,088.3	23,097.9	26,994.3	22,906.0	560.28%	18.72%
Total Lotteries	4,088.3	25,548.2	30,872.6	26,784.3	655.14%	20.18%
Casinos						
Nevada/NJ Slots	14,400.0	94,557.3	102,559.8	88,159.8	612.22%	19.54%
Nevada/NJ Tables	87,000.0	143,619.0	150,908.8	63,908.8	73.46%	5.13%
Cruise Ships		4,280.5	4,494.5	4,494.5	N/A	N/A
Riverboats		7,419.2	27,122.1	27,122.1	N/A	N/A
Other Land-Based Casinos		3,062.1	4,366.7	4,366.7	N/A	N/A
Other Commercial Gambling		379.2	410.0	410.0	N/A	N/A
Non-Casino Devices		3,838.3	7,413.4	7,413.4	N/A	N/A
Total Casinos	101,400.0	257,155.7	297,275.3	195,875.3	193.17%	10.27%
Legal Bookmaking						
Sports Books	415.2	1,800.8	2,006.3	1,591.1	383.25%	15.40%
Horse Books	122.8	307.5	251.0	128.2	104.42%	6.72%
Total Bookmaking	538.0	2,108.3	2,257.3	1,719.4	319.60%	13.93%
Card Rooms	1,000.0	8,428.1	8,451.1	7,451.1	745.11%	21.41%
Charitable Bingo	3,000.0	4,182.0	4,226.1	1,226.1	40.87%	3.16%
Charitable Games	1,200.0	4,703.7	4,886.4	3,686.4	307.20%	13.62%
Indian Reservations						
Class II		1,430.0	1,450.9	1,450.9	N/A	24.58% (2)
Class III		15,297.0	27,505.8	27,505.8	N/A	N/A
Total Indian Reservations		16,727.0	28,956.7	28,956.7	N/A	N/A
Grand Total	**$125,755.5**	**$336,662.4**	**$394,322.4**	**$268,566.9**	**213.56%**	**10.95%**

Notes:
Lottery handles for 1982 are for the twelve months ending June 30th.

Columns may not add to totals due to rounding.

(1) Average annual rate from 1983 to 1993.
(2) Average annual rate from 1985 to 1993.

Source: *International Gaming & Wagering Business*, September 5, 1994

TABLE 2.4
Trends in Gross Revenues (Consumer Spending), 1982 - 1993

(In $ millions)

	Gross Revenues (Spending) 1982	Gross Revenues (Spending) 1992 (Revised)	Gross Revenues (Spending) 1993	1982 - 1993 Gross Revenues Increase/(Decrease) Dollars	Percent	Average Annual Rate 1982-93
Pari-Mutuels						
Horses						
Tracks	$1,850.0	$1,921.3	$1,820.0	($30.0)	-1.62%	-0.15%
OTB	400.0	1,007.9	1,044.6	644.6	161.15%	9.12%
Total	2,250.0	2,929.2	2,864.6	614.6	27.32%	2.22%
Greyhounds						
Tracks	430.0	679.6	676.7	246.7	57.37%	4.21%
OTB		11.9	20.1	20.1	N/A	38.77% (1)
Total	430.0	691.5	696.7	266.7	62.03%	4.49%
Jai Alai	112.0	82.3	84.7	-27.3	-24.34%	-2.50%
Total Pari-Mutuels	2,792.0	3,702.9	3,646.1	854.1	30.59%	2.46%
Lotteries						
Video Lotteries		241.4	392.7	392.7	N/A	N/A
All Other Games	2,170.0	11,191.8	12,424.7	10,254.70	472.57%	17.19%
Total Lotteries	2,170.0	11,433.2	12,817.4	10,647.40	490.66%	17.52%
Casinos						
Nevada/NJ Slots	2,000.0	5,830.6	6,158.6	4,158.60	207.93%	10.77%
Nevada/NJ Tables	2,200.0	3,120.1	3,232.0	1,032.00	46.91%	3.56%
Cruise Ships		305.4	320.7	320.7	N/A	N/A
Riverboats		417.9	1,457.0	1,457.00	N/A	N/A
Other Land-Based Casinos		220.4	303.3	303.3	N/A	N/A
Other Commercial Gambling		126.9	143.2	143.2	N/A	N/A
Non-Casino Devices		566.2	922.7	922.7	N/A	N/A
Total Casinos	4,200.0	10,587.5	12,537.5	8,337.50	198.51%	10.45%
Legal Bookmaking						
Sports Books	7.7	50.6	75.0	67.3	871.34%	22.96%
Horse Books	18.0	46.8	40.0	22	121.99%	7.52%
Total Bookmaking	25.8	97.4	115.1	89.3	346.68%	14.58%
Card Rooms	50.0	660.8	662.4	612.4	1224.77%	26.48%
Charitable Bingo	780.0	1,033.5	1,037.0	257	32.95%	2.62%
Charitable Games	396.0	1,241.0	1,288.8	892.8	225.46%	11.32%
Indian Reservations						
Class II		429.0	435.3	435.3	N/A	22.21% (2)
Class III		1,202.6	2,159.6	2,159.60	N/A	N/A
Total Indian Reservations		1,631.6	2,594.9	2,594.90	N/A	N/A
Grand Total	$10,413.8	$30,387.9	$34,699.2	$24,285.4	233.21%	11.56%

Notes:
Lottery revenues for 1982 are for the twelve months ending June 30th.

Columns may not add to totals due to rounding.
(1) Average rate calculated from 1984 to 1993.
(2) Average rate calculated from 1985 to 1993.

Source: *International Gaming & Wagering Business*, August 5, 1994

Wagering Business estimated that Americans lost about $6.7 billion on illegal gambling, about 22 percent of all gambling losses that year.

GAMBLING ON INDIAN RESERVATIONS

The Indian Gaming Regulatory Act (PL 100-497) permits Native-American tribes to set up gambling on their reservations. Many tribes had already been holding bingo games on their reservations, but the new law gave Native Americans a chance to take advantage of the growing national interest in gambling. The law allowed tribes to make an agreement with the state where their reservations are to set up any kind of gambling they want on the reservation even though that kind of gambling (casinos, for instance) might be illegal everywhere else in the state. By 1993, according to the Bureau of Indian Affairs, 62 tribes in 18 states had agreements which permitted casino gambling.

The amount of money bet at Indian reservations has risen from nothing in 1982 to an estimated $29 billion in 1993. The reservation keeps about 9 percent of the handle — about $2.6 billion in 1993. These numbers are expected to continue increasing over the next few years.

TABLE 2.5

Market Shares (Revenues), 1993 vs. 1992	1992 Revenue Market Shares	1993 Revenue Market Shares	Increase/ (Decrease)
Riverboats	1.38%	4.20%	2.82%
Indian Class III	3.96%	6.22%	2.27%
Non-Casino Devices	1.86%	2.66%	0.80%
Video Lotteries	0.79%	1.13%	0.34%
Other Land-Based Casinos	0.73%	0.87%	0.15%
Sports Books	0.17%	0.22%	0.05%
Greyhound OTB	0.04%	0.06%	0.02%
Other Commercial Gambling	0.42%	0.41%	0.00%
Jai Alai	0.27%	0.24%	-0.03%
Horse Books	0.15%	0.12%	-0.04%
Cruise Ships	1.01%	0.92%	-0.08%
Indian Class II	1.41%	1.25%	-0.16%
Card Rooms	2.17%	1.91%	-0.27%
Greyhound Tracks	2.24%	1.95%	-0.29%
Horse OTB	3.32%	3.01%	-0.31%
Charitable Games	4.08%	3.71%	-0.37%
Charitable Bingo	3.40%	2.99%	-0.41%
Nevada/NJ Tables	10.27%	9.31%	-0.95%
All Other Lotteries	36.83%	35.81%	-1.02%
Horse Tracks	6.32%	5.25%	-1.08%
Nevada/NJ Slots	19.19%	17.75%	-1.44%
Total Indian Reservations	5.37%	7.48%	2.11%
Total Casinos	34.84%	36.13%	1.29%
Total Bookmaking	0.32%	0.33%	0.01%
Total Greyhounds	2.28%	2.01%	-0.27%
Total Lotteries	37.62%	36.94%	-0.69%
Total Horses	9.64%	8.26%	-1.38%
Total Pari-Mutuels	12.19%	10.51%	-1.68%

Source: *International Gaming & Wagering Business*, August 5, 1994

CHAPTER III

PARI-MUTUEL BETTING — HORSES, DOGS, AND JAI-ALAI

HOW PARI-MUTUEL BETTING WORKS

The term pari-mutuel betting is a type of betting in which bettors try to pick which horse or dog will win (first place), place (second place) or show (third place). Pari-mutuel betting also includes jai-alai, a game in which players use baskets strapped to their arms to catch and throw a hard ball against three walls and the floor of a court called a *fronton* (see below). The jai-alai handle is small in comparison to other pari-mutuel betting.

The money that is bet is collected and, after a percentage of money is taken out to pay taxes, to pay the purses (the prizes that go to the winning jai-alai players and owners of the winning horses or dogs), and to pay the track, the rest of the money is paid back to the bettors who have picked the winning dogs or horses. In

TABLE 3.1
1993 Handle by Industry and Change from 1992

(In $ millions)

	1993 Gross Wagering (Handle)	1992 - 1993 Gross Wagering Increase/(Decrease) Dollars	Percent
Pari-Mutuels			
Horses			
Tracks	$8,863.90	($517.90)	-5.50%
OTB	4,885.5	189.7	4.00%
Total	13,749.4	(328.3)	-2.30%
Greyhounds			
Tracks	3,168.8	(77.9)	-2.40%
OTB	94.7	35.6	60.30%
Total	3,263.5	(42.3)	-1.30%
Jai Alai	384.2	(41.7)	-9.80%
Total Pari-Mutuels	17,397.1	(412.3)	-2.30%
Lotteries			
Video Lotteries	3,878.3	1,428.0	58.30%
Other Games	26,994.3	3,896.4	16.90%
Total Lotteries	30,872.6	5,324.4	20.80%
Casinos			
Nevada/NJ Slots	102,559.8	8,002.4	8.50%
Nevada/NJ Tables	150,908.8	7,289.8	5.10%
Cruise Ships	4,494.5	214.0	5.00%
Riverboats	27,122.1	19,702.9	265.60%
Other Land-Based Casinos	4,366.7	1,304.6	42.60%
Other Commercial Gambling	410.0	30.8	8.10%
Non-Casino Devices	7,413.4	3,575.1	93.10%
Total Casinos	297,275.3	40,119.6	15.60%
Legal Bookmaking			
Sports Books	2,006.3	205.5	11.40%
Horse Books	251.0	(56.5)	-18.40%
Total Bookmaking	2,257.3	149.0	7.10%
Card Rooms	8,451.1	23.0	0.30%
Charitable Bingo	4,226.1	44.1	1.10%
Charitable Games	4,886.4	182.6	3.90%
Indian Reservations			
Class II	1,450.9	20.9	1.50%
Class III	27,505.8	12,208.8	79.80%
Total Indian Reservations	28,956.7	12,229.6	73.10%
Grand Total	$394,322.4	$57,660.0	17.10%

Columns may not add to totals due to rounding.

Source: *International Gaming & Wagering Business*, August 5, 1994

TABLE 3.2

	Live Racing Days					Live Races Run			
	Thoroughbred	Quarter Horse	Harness	Mixed	Total	Thoroughbred	Quarter Horse	Harness	Mixed	Total
Alabama	70				70	647				647
Arizona				281	281				2,700	2,700
Arkansas	62				62	615				615
California	466	143	107	117	833	4,457	1,779	1,319	1,425	8,980
Colorado				100	100				1,072	1,072
Connecticut	No Live Horse Racing Conducted									
Delaware	143		65		208	1,216		N/A	152	1,368
Florida	376		182		558	3,806		2,257		6,063
Idaho				110	110				1,074	1,074
Illinois	393		634		1,027	3,949		6,939		10,888
Iowa				60	60					
Kansas				63	63	398	151		642	642
Kentucky	310		76		386	2,956		776		3,732
Louisiana		91		469	560		910		4,690	5,600
Maine			226		226			N/A		N/A
Maryland	262		341		603	2,507		4,104		6,611
Massachusetts	165		199		364	1,412		N/A		1,412
Michigan	180		682	39	901	1,895		8,368	323	10,586
Montana				71	71				780	780
Nebraska	201	5			206	1,932	31			1,963
Nevada				15	15				146	146
New Hampshire	100		14		114	1,070		196		1,266
New Jersey	287		459		746	2,870		5,049		7,919
New Mexico				343	343	3,176	1,174			4,350
New York	461		1,057		1,518	N/A		N/A	N/A	N/A
North Dakota			3	10	13			N/A	N/A	N/A
Ohio	482	5	807		1,294	4,820	5	5,960		10,785
Oklahoma	119			245	364	1,183			2,619	3,802
Oregon				137	137				1,419	1,419
Pennsylvania	497		383		880	4,721		4,979		9,700
Rhode Island	No Live Horse Racing Conducted									
South Dakota				15	15				177	177
Texas				351	351				3,784	3,784
Vermont			10		10			111		111
Washington	263	13		7	283	2,665	125		62	2,852
West Virginia	416				416	4,130				4,130
Wyoming				49	49				556	556
Totals	**5,253**	**267**	**5,245**	**2,482**	**13,237**	**50,425**	**4,175**	**40,058**	**21,621**	**116,279**

Note: Although totals are given, please note that the number of races is not available in some jurisdictions. In Ohio, the number of races excludes harness racing fairs.

Source: *Pari-Mutuel Racing—1993*, Association of Racing Commissioners International, Inc (Lexington, KY, 1994)

1993, bettors placed $17.4 billion on horses, dogs, and jai-alai games. Table 3.1 shows a break-down of gross wagering (the handle) on pari-mutuel betting in 1993.

How A Person Bets

The amount a bettor wins depends on how much is bet on a given race. If the winner of the race was heavily favored (a lot of people thought the horse would win), then the payoff is not very large because so many people had bet on the same horse. If the winner was a "long shot," a horse few people expected to win, then the payoff will be very great. For example, if a horse is a 2-to-1 favorite, it means that for every dollar bet on that horse, $2 has been bet on the other horses. A lot of people think this horse will win, so it is considered a favorite. If this horse wins, the winning bettors will get only about $2 back for every dollar they bet.

If people do not think the horse is very fast, and few people bet on it, it might have 30-to-1 odds. That means that for every $1 bet on this horse, $30 was bet on all the others. A lot of people do not think this horse will win, so they are betting on other horses. If it does, the few bettors who won will divide all the money of those who picked the other horses. The winning bettor will get about $30 for every $1 he or she bet.

The smallest amount a person can bet in pari-mutuel betting is $2. A person may bet as much as he or she likes, but the wager has to be in amounts of $2, $5, $10, $50, or $100. That means a person could bet $65 ($50+$10+$5), but he or she could not bet $67 or $50.55.

HOW OLD DO YOU HAVE TO BE TO GAMBLE?

Pari-mutuel racing is legal in all but seven states (Alaska, Georgia, Hawaii, Mississippi, North Carolina, South Carolina, and Utah). In most states where pari-mutuel gambling is legal, a person must be 18 years old to bet, although in Illinois a 17-year-old may wager. In Nebraska, Wyoming, and Macon County, Alabama, the age is 19 years, while in Birmingham, Alabama, New York State, and Texas the legal age for betting is 21 years. However, most states do not have an age limit on simply going to a racetrack to watch the horse race or dog race, although several states do require that a minor come with an adult.

HORSE RACING — THE SPORT OF KINGS

Horse racing has been around for a very long time. More than 6,000 years ago, the Sumerians in the ancient Middle East ran chariot races. "Flat racing," in which the rider sits directly on the horse, took place around 3000 years ago. The first recorded horse race took place in Greece about 660 B.C. Horse racing became one of the favorite pastimes of the British kings and nobles between 1100 and 1600, and because of that became known as the "Sport of Kings."

TABLE 3.3

On-Track Attendance

	Thoroughbred	Quarter Horse	Harness	Mixed	Total
Alabama	93,224				93,224
Arizona				669,117	669,117
Arkansas	1,078,352				1,078,352
California	4,601,598	417,776	194,356	464,793	5,678,523
Colorado				173,602	173,602
Connecticut					
Delaware	463,499		67,302		530,801
Florida	1,926,261		482,631		2,408,892
Idaho				171,893	171,893
Illinois	2,222,732		1,559,808		3,782,540
Iowa				292,051	292,051
Kansas				98,897	98,897
Kentucky	1,986,990		130,243		2,117,233
Louisiana		105,802		926,126	1,031,928
Maine			N/A		N/A
Maryland	2,549,412		696,362		3,245,774
Massachusetts	1,107,305		251,048		1,358,353
Michigan	732,390		1,655,049	27,231	2,414,670
Montana				N/A	N/A
Nebraska	582,065	1,080			583,145
Nevada				N/A	N/A
New Hampshire	345,073		N/A		345,073
New Jersey	1,765,376		2,115,121		3,880,497
New Mexico				1,014,508	1,014,508
New York	3,581,637		1,822,845		5,204,482
North Dakota			N/A	N/A	N/A
Ohio	1,647,364	13,193	1,824,270		3,484,827
Oklahoma	936,392			623,155	1,559,547
Oregon				N/A	N/A
Pennsylvania	2,164,638		577,210		2,741,848
Rhode Island					
South Dakota				8,306	8,306
Texas				775,711	775,711
Vermont			N/A		N/A
Washington	185,681	N/A			185,681
West Virginia	758,205				758,205
Wyoming				N/A	N/A
Totals	**28,728,194**	**537,851**	**11,176,245**	**5,245,390**	**45,687,680**

On-Track Average Attendance

	Thoroughbred	Quarter Horse	Harness	Mixed	Total
Alabama	1,332				1,332
Arizona				2,381	2,381
Arkansas	17,393				17,393
California	9,875	2,922	1,816	3,973	6,817
Colorado				1,736	1,736
Connecticut					
Delaware	3,241		1,035		2,552
Florida	5,123		2,652		4,317
Idaho				1,563	1,563
Illinois	5,656		2,460		3,683
Iowa				4,868	4,868
Kansas				1,570	1,570
Kentucky	6,410		1,714		5,485
Louisiana		1,163		1,975	1,843
Maine			N/A		N/A
Maryland	9,731		2,042		5,383
Massachusetts	6,711		1,262		3,732
Michigan	4,069		2,427	698	2,680
Montana				N/A	N/A
Nebraska	2,096	216			2,831
Nevada				N/A	N/A
New Hampshire	3,451		N/A		3,027
New Jersey	6,151		4,906		5,202
New Mexico				2,958	2,958
New York	7,759		1,535		3,428
North Dakota			N/A	N/A	N/A
Ohio	3,418	2,639	2,251		2,693
Oklahoma	7,869			2,543	4,284
Oregon				N/A	N/A
Pennsylvania	4,355		1,507		3,116
Rhode Island					
South Dakota				554	554
Texas				2,210	2,210
Vermont			N/A		N/A
Washington	706	N/A			656
West Virginia	1,823				1,823
Wyoming				N/A	N/A
Totals	**6,469**	**2,093**	**2,131**	**2,113**	**3,452**

Note: In some states (indicated by "N/A"), attendance is not collected by the Commission; attendance counts in Arizona include major meetings only.

Source: *Pari-Mutuel Racing —1993*, Association of Racing Commissioners International, Inc (Lexington, KY, 1994)

Horse racing was very popular in colonial America among the rich. The first race track in America was the Newmarket Course, built in 1665 in Hempstead, New York. By 1800, horse racing was common at county fairs, mainly in Maryland, Virginia, and Kentucky. The first big track with a grandstand large enough to seat thousands of people was New York's Belmont Park which opened in 1905. In 1934, California's Santa Anita Race Track began horse racing. The largest track in the United States, New York's Aqueduct, opened in 1959.

Types of Horse Racing Events

The three types of horse racing are thoroughbred, harness, and quarter horse racing. Thoroughbred racing is by far the most popular form, followed by harness and then quarter horse racing. A thoroughbred horse is taller and has longer legs than other horses. The rider, or jockey, sits on or mounts a saddle that is directly on the horse's back.

In harness racing, the rider sits in a one-horse, two-wheel carriage, called a sulky, and directs the horse around the track. The horses are trained to be trotters or pacers. A trotter runs moving the left front and right rear legs forward almost at the same time, and then the right front and left rear legs move forward. A pacer moves both left legs forward at the same time, and then moves both right legs forward.

The quarter horse (the word *quarter* refers to the quarter-mile race it runs) is a very swift horse that can run faster than other types of horses over a short distance. Unlike the thoroughbreds, trotters, and pacers, quarter horses can be used for farm work and transportation.

Number of Horse Races

In 1993, 116,279 horse races were held in the United States. Most were either thoroughbred (50,425) or harness (40,058) races. Only 4,175 quarter horse races took place. Illinois (10,888), Ohio (10,785), and Michigan (10,586) had the most races (Table 3.2).

Attendance

In 1993, almost 45.7 million people went to horse racing events. Thoroughbred racing was the most popular with a total attendance of almost 29 million people. Harness racing attracted more than 11 million while quarter horse racing events drew 537,851. (See Table 3.3.)

Horse racing is not as popular as it once was and attendance has been falling over the past few years. In 1990, more than 63.8 million people went to the race tracks, but by 1993, that number had fallen sharply to fewer than 46 million. According to experts in the gaming business, competition from other gambling activities, especially casinos, has drawn some people away from the tracks. In addition, off-track betting and simulcasting of races (see below) make it easier for people to place bets without actually going to the track where the races are being run.

TABLE 3.4
HORSE RACING IN THE UNITED STATES

HORSE RACING REVENUE TO GOVERNMENT
1934 - 1993

1993	$471,735,474	1978	673,063,831	1963	316,570,791	1948	95,803,364
1992	491,259,606	1977	700,239,986	1962	287,930,030	1947	97,926,984
1991	523,249,392	1976	714,629,120	1961	264,853,077	1946	94,035,859
1990	623,839,806	1975	780,081,431	1960	258,039,385	1945	65,265,405
1989	584,888,183	1974	645,980,984	1959	243,388,655	1944	55,971,233
1988	596,202,319	1973	585,201,524	1958	222,049,651	1943	38,194,727
1987	608,351,461	1972	531,404,550	1957	216,747,621	1942	22,005,278
1986	587,357,677	1971	512,838,417	1956	207,456,272	1941	21,128,173
1985	625,159,697	1970	486,403,097	1955	186,989,588	1940	16,145,182
1984	650,262,852	1969	461,498,886	1954	178,015,828	1939	10,369,807
1983	641,387,176	1968	426,856,448	1953	167,426,465	1938	9,576,335
1982	652,888,463	1967	394,381,913	1952	142,489,696	1937	8,434,792
1981	680,199,584	1966	388,452,125	1951	117,250,564	1936	8,611,538
1980	712,727,523	1965	369,892,036	1950	98,366,167	1935	8,386,255
1979	680,919,798	1964	350,095,928	1949	95,327,053	1934	6,024,193

Source: *Pari-Mutuel Racing—1993*, Association of Racing Commissioners International, Inc (Lexington, KY, 1994)

The Horse Racing Handle and Where It Went

Bettors placed more than $13 billion in bets on the horses in 1993. New York took in $2.85 billion and California took in $2.45 billion. The state governments got $325 million mostly in tax money. The total amount of state and federal government revenues from horse racing in 1993 was almost $472 million (Table 3.4). The owners of the winning horses got a little more than $850 million in prize money (called "the purse") for winning the races. In most horse races, the first four horses get prize money.

DOG RACING — THE SPORT OF QUEENS

Dog racing came out of a hunting sport called "coursing." A hare (a field animal like a rabbit but larger) would be released, and then a pair of greyhound dogs would be turned loose to catch the hare. Coursing was very popular when Queen Elizabeth I ruled England in the last half of the 1500s. For this reason, it became known as the "Sport of Queens."

The modern version of dog racing developed from a coursing event in South Dakota in 1904. Owen Patrick Smith, who was the host of the event, loved the sport, but he hated the killing of the hare. Smith developed the mechanical lure. The dogs chase a fake hare that is attached to the inside rail of the race track as it lures or leads them around the track.

Dog racing normally refers to racing of greyhound dogs, a lean, long-legged breed known for speed in running. Even though casino and other forms of gambling have

TABLE 3.5

GREYHOUND RACING

	Attendance				Number of Live Races		
	On-Track	Average	ITW	OTW	Matinees	Evenings	Total
Birmingham, AL	779,227	1,808	3,182		1,946	4,187	6,133
Greene County, AL	247,707	541					5,954
Macon County, AL	867,742	1,725			2,692	3,900	6,592
Mobile County, AL	466,826	1,042			2,054	3,770	5,824
Alabama Total	2,361,502	1,283	3,182		N/A	N/A	24,503
Arizona	1,061,157	886			4,964	9,251	14,215
Arkansas	1,202,414	2,926			2,080	3,471	5,551
Colorado	836,356	987	394,120	61,449			10,953
Connecticut	421,685	911					6,442
Florida	7,629,446	1,660			22,011	41,521	63,532
Idaho	249,610	821					4,880
Iowa	659,580	777					11,164
Kansas	1,553,001	1,767			5,644	6,325	11,969
Massachusetts	2,136,600	1,942					13,193
New Hampshire	652,431	653			8,220	6,765	14,985
Oregon	N/A						2,168
Rhode Island	N/A				3,393	2,678	6,071
South Dakota				74,257			
Texas	2,967,048	2,214	12,923		5,968	10,942	16,910
West Virginia	908,386	1,203			2,687	8,509	11,196
Wisconsin	2,357,043	1,422			11,385	11,574	22,959
Totals	24,996,259	1,391	410,225	135,706	N/A	N/A	240,671

Source: *Pari-Mutuel Racing—1993*, Association of Racing Commissioners International, Inc (Lexington, KY, 1994)

drawn bettors away from the greyhound tracks, the sport is still popular. In 1990, it was the fifth largest spectator sport. Almost 25 million people attended the 240,671 greyhound races held in 1993 (Table 3.5). The greyhound racing handle totaled $3.26 billion in 1993, and governments got $194 million, mostly tax revenues, while the owners of the winning dogs received $131 million in prize money.

JAI-ALAI

The word jai-alai means "merry-festival." Jai-alai is a very fast game in which the players use large, curved baskets, strapped to their arms to catch and whip a small, hard ball (made of goat hide) against three walls and the floor of a huge playing court called a *fronton*. The game is similar to handball or racquetball played in America. Jai-alai was invented in the 1600s by the Basques, a people who live in northern Spain and southern France. A popular game in Latin America, it is played in only three states (Connecticut, Florida, and Rhode Island) in the United States.

In 1993, 4.2 million people watched 43,056 jai-alai games played at 3,200 performances. Almost two thirds (62 percent) of the games, performances, and attendance took place in Florida. The pari-mutuel handle totalled a little more than $384 million, and total government revenues were $26 million. Hampered by player strikes beginning in the late 1980s, the jai-alai industry has not been doing well, and the handle has been decreasing.

OFF-TRACK BETTING (OTB)

At one time, a person who wanted to make a legal bet on a horse race or dog race had to go to a racetrack to do it. However, in 1970, New York State passed a law allowing off-track betting (OTB). New York City opened the first off-track betting parlor in 1971. Off-track betting is just what the name says — a person places a bet on a horse or a dog race at some place other than the race track. OTB bets are usually placed at a track branch office or a betting shop or parlor. Some states permit the bettor to call in his or her bet over the telephone. Ten states (California, Connecticut, Illinois, Kentucky, Louisiana, New York, Oregon, Pennsylvania, Washington, and Wyoming) permit off-track betting.

Simulcasting

Simulcasting, another kind of off-track betting (OTB), can take place even at a track where the race is not being run. The race is shown live on television at another race track, or at a gambling parlor, or at a simulcasting theater where the race is shown on a big screen at the same time the race is happening. People then can bet on the race before it is run just as if they were at the race track. In 1993, more than $76 million was bet on simulcast horse races, and almost $4 billion was spent on off-track betting. The handle for simulcast greyhound races was $3.7 million. Off-track wagering took in $94.7 million. The money earned from off-track betting is divided among the racetrack owners, the OTB operators, and the state and local governments.

CHAPTER IV

CASINO GAMBLING

A casino is any room or rooms in which gambling takes place. When most people think of casinos, they imagine the casinos in Las Vegas they have seen on television or in the movies. For many years, casinos were legal only in Las Vegas, Nevada. In 1977, the State of New Jersey passed a law to allow gambling in Atlantic City.

Over the past few years, as state and local governments have needed more money, many have turned to gambling to raise funds. Lotteries have been the most frequently chosen form of gambling to be introduced, but several states have legalized casinos. Casinos can now be found in Deadwood, South Dakota, and Cripple Creek, Colorado. Other casinos now float up and down the Mississippi and Missouri Rivers and out into the Gulf of Mexico and the Atlantic and Pacific Oceans. The City of New Orleans will soon open a giant casino in hopes of drawing even more people to the city. Many Native-American tribes have opened casinos on their reservations.

FIRST, CASINOS IN NEVADA

Casinos have been part of life in Nevada ever since the first settlers arrived in search of gold. In 1869, the Nevada legislature legalized gambling and, except for a few pe-

```
                        TABLE 4.1

        NEVADA COMBINED INCOME STATEMENT - SUMMARY

Fiscal Year 1994
Statewide Casinos
With Gaming Revenue of $1,000,000 and over

AMOUNTS REPRESENT 207 LOCATION(S).


                                                DOLLARS      PCT
REVENUE
   GAMING . . . . . . . . . . . . . . . . . . 6,504,348,451  59.7
   ROOMS  . . . . . . . . . . . . . . . . . . 1,586,137,853  14.6
   FOOD . . . . . . . . . . . . . . . . . . . 1,299,990,707  11.9
   BEVERAGE . . . . . . . . . . . . . . . . .   587,519,449   5.4
   OTHER  . . . . . . . . . . . . . . . . . .   918,835,264   8.4
      TOTAL REVENUE . . . . . . . . . . . . .10,896,831,724 100.0
```
Source: *Nevada Gaming Abstract — 1994*, State Gaming Control Board (Carson City, NV, December 1994)

FIGURE 4.1

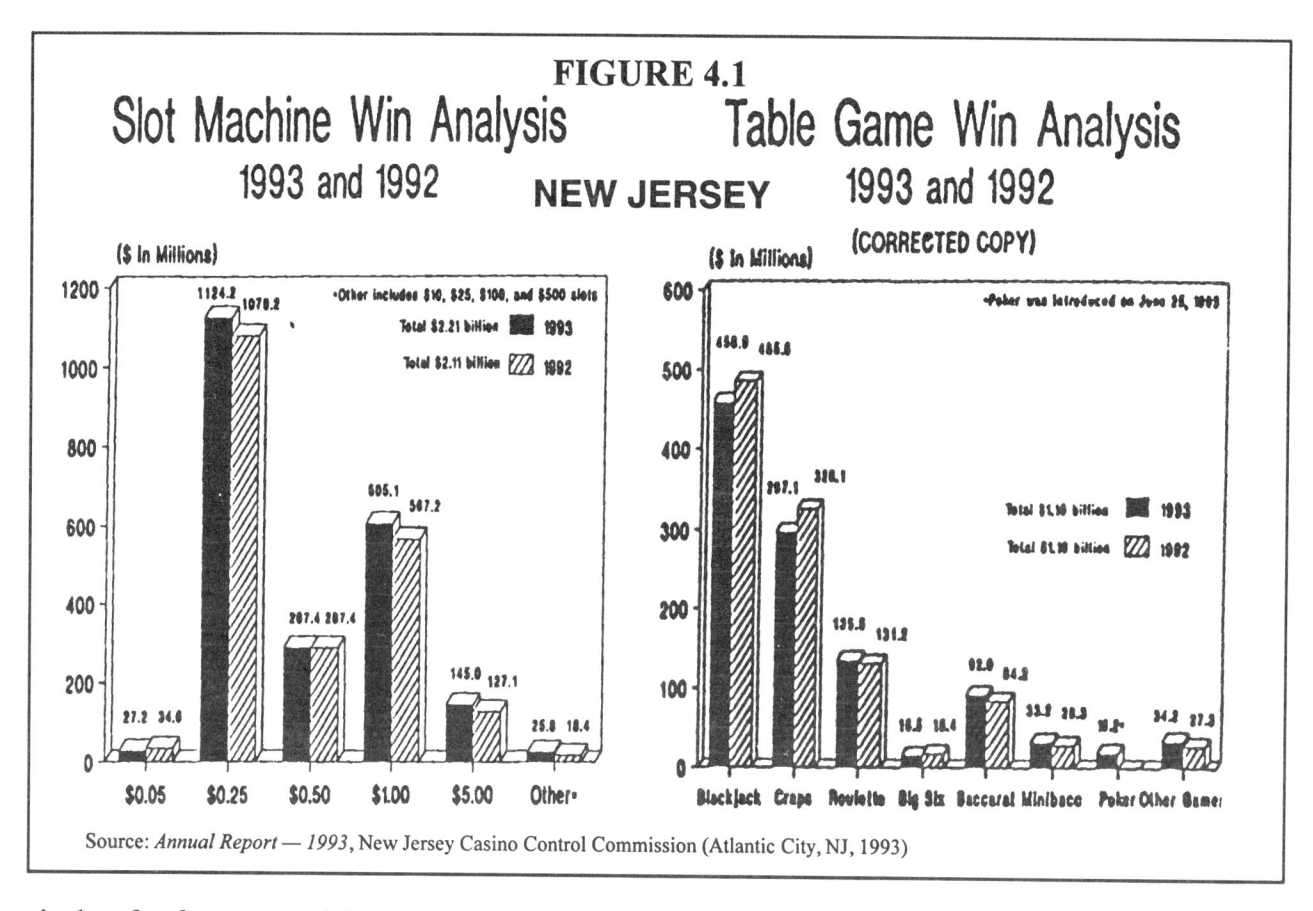

Slot Machine Win Analysis 1993 and 1992 — **NEW JERSEY** — **Table Game Win Analysis 1993 and 1992** (CORRECTED COPY)

Source: *Annual Report — 1993*, New Jersey Casino Control Commission (Atlantic City, NJ, 1993)

riods of reform, gambling has been legal in Nevada ever since. Today, gambling is the most important business in the state.

AND THEN NEW JERSEY

One hundred years ago, Atlantic City, New Jersey, was one of the most famous seaside vacation spots in the United States. Thousands of tourists walked along the famous Boardwalk, a wide, wooden sidewalk-like bridge placed just above the sand. By the 1950s, Atlantic City was no longer popular and the local economy was depressed (very bad). In an effort to improve the wealth of Atlantic City, the State of New Jersey legalized gambling in the city on June 2, 1977. All tax monies gotten from gambling are to be used for social programs like helping the elderly.

NOW CASINOS ARE ALMOST EVERYWHERE

During the 1980s and 1990s, many state and local communities were having trouble finding enough money to operate. Raising taxes was not popular, and so they looked for another way to collect money. Many states saw legalized casino gambling as a way to raise the needed money. The state would permit gambling and then tax the gambling monies by taking a percentage of the money bet. The state would also charge for the licenses that the gambling casinos had to pay in order to operate within the state.

By the early 1990s, card rooms (where players could gamble on card games) were booming in California, Oregon, Washington, and Montana. Other gamblers were betting in casinos in South Dakota and Colorado while casinos, located on riverboats based in Iowa, Illinois, Mississippi, and Louisiana, were floating up and down the Mississippi River.

Meanwhile, dozens of Native American tribes opened casinos on their reservations. At sea, many cruise lines added or expanded casino operations on their cruise ships to earn more money. Other cruise ships were simply floating gambling casinos which sailed out into the Gulf of Mexico or the Atlantic and Pacific Oceans outside the United States so that their passengers could gamble.

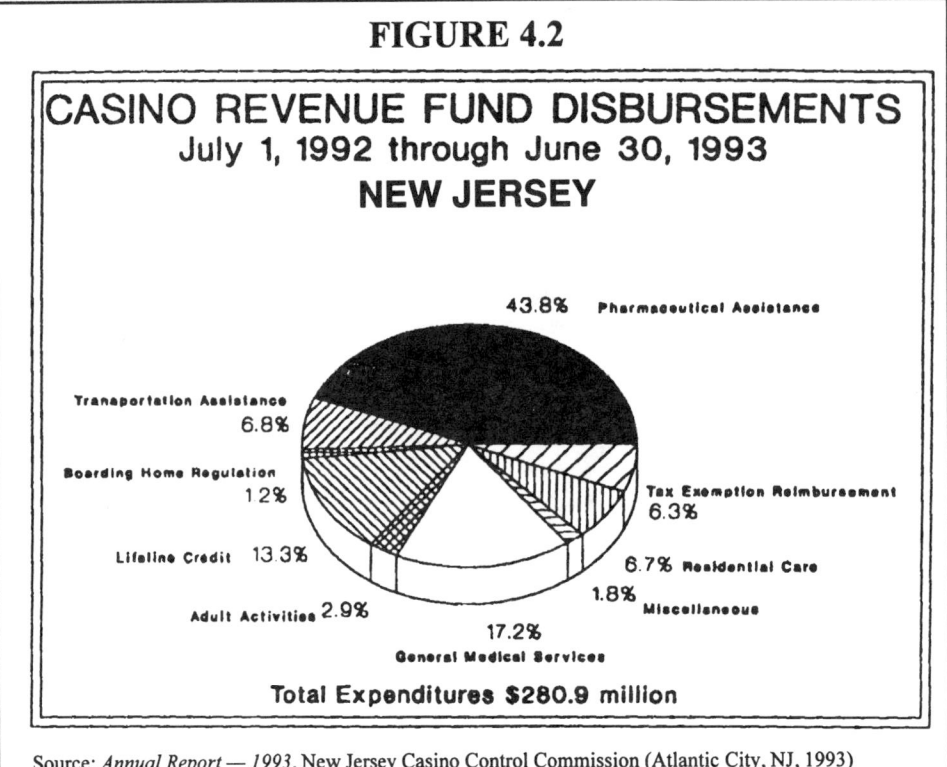

FIGURE 4.2

CASINO REVENUE FUND DISBURSEMENTS
July 1, 1992 through June 30, 1993
NEW JERSEY

- 43.8% Pharmaceutical Assistance
- Transportation Assistance 6.8%
- Boarding Home Regulation 1.2%
- Lifeline Credit 13.3%
- Adult Activities 2.9%
- General Medical Services 17.2%
- Miscellaneous 1.8%
- Residential Care 6.7%
- Tax Exemption Reimbursement 6.3%

Total Expenditures $280.9 million

Source: *Annual Report — 1993*, New Jersey Casino Control Commission (Atlantic City, NJ, 1993)

CASINO GAMES

Slot Machines

Slot machines are similar to vending machines. The player puts some coins in the slot, pulls a lever or pushes a button, and then hopes to win a lot of money from the machine. Bettors can put in as little as 5 cents or can try their luck on the $1 machines. The average machine returns about 85 cents for every dollar that is bet. The other 15 cents is divided between the government, which taxes the amount bet, and the owners of the casino.

Table Games

Table games include twenty-one (also known as blackjack), craps, roulette, and bingo. Not every gambling casino has every game, but the larger casinos will have most of the table games.

CASINO REVENUES

In 1993, Americans spent about $297.3 billion on casino games and slot machines. The casinos won a record $14.7 billion. That is more money than Americans spent on movies, theater, opera, and classical and popular music concerts. Almost all of it was bet on table games in Nevada and New Jersey ($150.9 billion) and slot machines in Nevada and New Jersey ($102.5 billion). Since the house (the owners of the gambling casinos), on average, keeps more of the money bet on slot machines (6 percent in 1993) than they do on table games (2.10 percent), slot machines earn more money for the casino owners. In 1993, Nevada and New Jersey casinos earned $6.15 billion from the slot machines and $3.2 billion from the table games.

Nevada

In 1993, the 207 major casinos in the state of Nevada (those casinos that took in more than $1 million that year) produced $10.9 billion in gross revenues. Of this amount, almost 60 percent ($6.5 billion) came from gambling, mostly from slot machines ($4 billion) and table games ($2.1 billion). While most of the money comes from gambling, some money comes in from room charges (15 percent), food (12 percent), and drinks (6 percent). (See Table 4.1.)

Gambling is a business, just like selling cars or corn flakes. Most hotels will give away food, drinks, rooms, and entertainment to heavy gamblers so they will come to Las Vegas, have a good time, stay a long time, and keep gambling. These free drinks, rooms, etc., are called complimentary expenses or "comps."

The hotels are getting bigger and bigger, and the owners are trying to make them more exciting. In 1989 and 1990, the huge, 3,000-room Mirage Hotel and the even larger, 4,000-room Excalibur, the biggest hotel in the world at the time, opened in Las Vegas. In 1993, three more gigantic hotels/casinos/tourist attractions opened: the Luxor Las Vegas, a 20-story, glass-covered pyramid; Treasure Island Resort, three 36-story towers with 2,900 rooms; and the MGM Grand Hotel in four 30-story towers with 5,005 rooms and a casino as big as four football fields.

Making Las Vegas a Family Place

The competition between the casinos is very great, and each casino is trying to do something to attract customers. The Mirage Hotel has a man-made volcano that erupts outside and a huge aquarium filled with tropical fish, including sharks and manta rays, inside. The Excalibur looks like a medieval castle, and the hosts wear medieval costumes. The telephone operators tell the guests to "Have a royal day." (See Figure 4.3.)

The MGM Grand has an amusement park almost as big as Disneyland and a huge child care center so that parents can leave their children with an adult while they go off to play the slot machines or the roulette table. Treasure Island Resort faces Buccaneer Bay, a theme park where two 90-foot ships do battle every hour. The owners of the larger casinos are trying to make Las Vegas a vacation spot for the whole family where the children, not just the parents, can have a good time.

FIGURE 4.3

THE EXCALIBUR HOTEL, LAS VEGAS, NEVADA

New Jersey

New Jersey permits casino gambling only in Atlantic City. The 12 casinos there grossed $3.3 billion in 1993. As shown in Figure 4.1, slot machines took in the most money with the $.25 slots bringing in the most and the $1.00 slots, next. Of the table games, blackjack was the most popular, with craps next, and roulette, third. New games introduced in 1993 were poker, which brought in about $10 million its first year, and keno, which was being tested for popularity in the casinos for the first time in 1994. Simulcasting of horse races was also added in 1993 with five casinos opening the attraction by the end of the year.

Atlantic City casinos have had some hard times. The depressed economy in the Northeast led many people to gamble less. Donald Trump, whose Trump Organization owns three casinos, has had many financial problems, mainly because his casinos have not earned as much money as planned. Also, many gamblers who come to gamble for a few hours on one day do not stay overnight in the hotels or spend money on other things. By introducing new games and allowing 24-hour-a-day gambling, the New Jersey Casino Control Commission hopes that Atlantic City will revive and prosper.

New Jersey Casino Revenue Fund

When New Jersey legalized gambling, it set up the Casino Revenue Fund to finance programs to help New Jersey's elderly and disabled people. The 12 operating casinos are taxed 8 percent of their "win" each month. (The "win" is the amount the casinos keep after all bets have been paid but before any other expenses are taken out.) In 1993, the Fund earned $258 million, although it actually spent more ($280.9 million) because of money left over from 1992. Figure 4.2 shows how the money was spent.

CASINO GAMBLING SPREADS ACROSS THE COUNTRY

Recreating the Wild, Wild West

Many states in the Midwest and West had economic problems during the 1980s and into the 1990s. They began looking for a new way to both raise money and bring tourists to their states. As a result, the voters of South Dakota approved casino gambling in the town of Deadwood, where the famous cowboy, Wild Bill Haycock, was killed while playing cards. The town has become a gambling center. Gambling supporters had expected betting to be around $4 million per year, but *International Gaming & Wagering Business* magazine estimated the take for the first year at about $295 million. Following Las Vegas' lead of creating family resorts instead of mere casinos, the Dunbar resort in Deadwood is scheduled to open in 1997 with 320 rooms and, among other things, a fitness center, a movie theater, a bowling alley, swimming pools, tennis courts, an 18-hole golf course, and a kids' camp that is more like an adventure land.

In Colorado, casinos have sprung up in the old mining towns of Central City, Black Hawk, and Cripple Creek. In the 1800s, gold and silver miners used to come to these towns to gamble. There was so much betting that gamblers would set up roulette tables in the streets. After the mining stopped, these towns almost became "ghost towns" as most people moved on. Now many thousands of people go there to gamble. A person can bet as often as he or she wants to, but bets in both South Dakota and Colorado are limited to $5 each bet.

Riverboat Gambling

Back in the 1800s, riverboats sailed up and down the larger rivers of the United States — the Ohio, Missouri, and Mississippi. Almost every passenger boat had a casino where people could spend their time gambling. Many states that are located on the Missouri or Mississippi River have brought back riverboat gambling. In 1991, the State of Iowa passed a law permitting riverboat gambling. Since then, five more states have permitted riverboat casinos: Missouri, Illinois, Indiana, Mississippi, and Louisiana.

Most of the riverboats range in size from 200 to 300 feet long and 45 to 95 feet wide.

The *President* sailing out of Davenport, Iowa, is 300 feet long, has a casino of 27,000 square feet, 669 slot machines, and 38 gaming tables. The smaller *Par-A-Dice* out of Peoria, Illinois, is 228 feet long, has 12,500 square feet of casino space with 478 slot machines and 40 tables.

Betting losses on the Iowa riverboats are limited to $200 a cruise. Across the river in Illinois, gamblers can bet as much as they like. Missouri, taking applications for riverboat licenses, has a $500 limit. Louisiana approved riverboat gambling in 1991 and will allow 15 boats on the 11 lakes and rivers. With a few exceptions (mainly video poker which limits bets to $2 and jackpots to $500), there will be no limits on betting or losses.

Observers expect most, if not all, 15 boats to be operating in the New Orleans area. These riverboats are expected to be much larger than the ones sailing out from Iowa and Illinois, probably as large as 3,000 feet and able to hold 2,500 to 3,000 passengers. The Louisiana economy has been depressed, and state leaders hope that riverboat gambling will attract thousands of tourists with millions of dollars to help the economy. With the riverboats and the new land-based casino, they hope that New Orleans will become the next Las Vegas.

Deep-Water Cruising

Gambling does not take place just on riverboats. Gamblers may board the *Pride of Galveston*, *LA Cruise*, and *Europa Jet*, based out of Texas and Mississippi, and take a three- to five-hour trip out into the Gulf of Mexico. Or they may travel to several Florida ports and get on one of several ships which cruise out into international waters or sail to the Bahamas. When the ship is in international waters, gamblers can bet at the ship's casinos and slot machines until the boat returns to U.S. waters.

Regular Cruises

Almost all major cruise ships offer gambling as entertainment for their passengers along with shows, dining, dancing, and shuffleboard. The Carnival Cruise Lines *Ecstasy*, a very large cruise ship, has 226 slot machines, 20 blackjack tables, 3 roulette wheels, 3 crap tables, and 3 poker tables. The cruise lines say that gambling is just one thing for people to do on cruises and not the most important thing.

Cruise companies want people to have a good time on their ships and to leave feeling happy. If passengers were to lose a lot of money, they would not remember the cruise trip fondly and might not come back or tell their friends what a wonderful time they had. Therefore, most cruise ships have a loss-limit of $100 to $200, so that no one will lose too much money. *International Gaming & Wagering Business* magazine reported that United States-based deep-water cruise ships earned an estimated $321 million in 1993.

Card Rooms

Card rooms are small gambling parlors where people can come to play cards, usually poker and blackjack, with other people for money. Public card rooms have been legal in California since the Gold Rush days. Currently, more than 300 licensed gambling parlors with over 2,000 tables are operating in California. The State of Washington has more than 80 clubs and limits bets to $10 per bet. Montana has more than 50 small clubs and limits the betting to $300 per pot. North Dakota has about 20 clubs, with most of the earnings going to charity.

Oregon permits "social gambling" — poker and blackjack games with small amounts of money at risk — in taverns and bars. Card rooms can also be found in Deadwood, South Dakota, and in Central City, Black Hawk, and Cripple Creek, Colorado. The card parlors usually earn money by charging the players for every hour or every hand they play. Card tables are also found in Nevada and Atlantic City, but they earn far less money than the slot machines or casino tables. As a result, there are only about 500 tables in all of Nevada.

A GROWING BUSINESS

In only a few years, casino gambling has spread from only two states to where it has been approved, in some form, in 14 states. (This does not include gambling on Native American Reservations. Gambling on reservations is covered in Chapter II.) Many states see gambling as a way to improve their economy and raise tax money. Many gaming business people believe there is a large demand for casino gambling — they think many Americans would go to a casino to gamble for entertainment if they were given the opportunity. The early successes of gambling in South Dakota and Colorado, of riverboat gambling on the Mississippi and Missouri, and the increases in casino gambling on cruise ships would seem to show that they are right.

CHAPTER V

LOTTERIES

A lottery is a game in which the players buy a numbered ticket and hope to win a prize if their number is the one drawn from among all of those who have bought tickets for the lottery. In instant lotteries, the bettor wins if the ticket has a number on it that has already been set as a winning number. Raffles are also a form of lottery, but the winner usually wins some type of product, a car, for example, instead of money. Raffles are usually held by churches or charitable organizations and normally are very small. As of 1993, lotteries were legal in 37 states (although only 36 states held them), Washington, DC, the Virgin Islands, and Puerto Rico. (See Table 5.1 for gross wagering totals for states that allow lotteries and other gambling.)

A PART OF AMERICAN HISTORY

Lotteries have been a part of American life since the settlement of Jamestown, Virginia, which was paid for by a lottery. Before the colonial governments (the governments in the colonies before the American Revolution) set up regular tax systems, many used lotteries to help pay for roads, schools, and universities. Many churches were also built from money raised through lotteries. Some of the nation's most famous banks, including the Chase Manhattan Bank and First City National Bank of New York, were founded by people who ran lotteries.

Many lotteries were not honestly run and some lottery managers stole the money. This sort of dishonesty led many people to oppose the lotteries and, by 1840, most northern states had outlawed them. By 1860, many western and southern states had abolished lotteries. Between 1860 and 1895, the federal government passed laws which made it impossible for lotteries to operate and, by the end of the 1800s, virtually no legal lotteries operated in the United States.

NEW LOTTERIES BEGIN

In 1964, following some changes in the federal law, the state of New Hampshire became the first state in the 20th century to legalize lottery games. New York began a state lottery in 1967 and New Jersey followed in 1971. Lotteries, however, did not spread across the country until the 1980s. The federal government began requiring the state governments to pay for many of the services the federal government used to pay for. At the same time, many citizens were getting upset about paying high taxes.

TABLE 5.1

1993 Gross Wagering by State

(In $ millions)

	Total Pari-Mutuels	Total Lotteries	Casinos & Devices[1]	Total Bookmaking	Card Rooms	Charitable Bingo[2]	Charitable Games[2]	Total[1]
Alabama	$386.5					$55.5		$442.0
Alaska						50.2	$176.7	226.9
Arizona	244.0	$284.1				50.8	67.6	646.5
Arkansas	317.4							317.4
California	2,456.7	1,836.3			$7,500.0	338.5	543.8	12,675.3
Colorado	209.3	281.0	$3,856.0			64.7	171.4	4,582.4
Connecticut	345.1	507.0				32.9	28.5	913.4
Delaware	89.7	100.9				11.1	17.1	218.8
DC		204.9				5.8	2.9	213.7
Florida	1,736.2	2,297.2				183.3	137.2	4,354.0
Georgia		557.4				68.4	68.4	694.3
Idaho	36.6	71.7						108.3
Illinois	1,282.0	1,507.9	11,575.1			157.1	107.7	14,629.8
Indiana		567.1				49.1	100.6	1,366.6
Iowa	96.5	218.0	649.8			52.8	6.8	374.1
Kansas	235.3	141.0				30.3	12.7	419.3
Kentucky	501.6	500.5				50.3		1,052.5
Louisiana	497.3	401.7	4,191.2			179.2	243.1	5,512.4
Maine	31.8	130.6				22.9	20.2	205.5
Maryland	532.8	970.8	89.6		157.6	79.1	121.5	1,951.4
Massachusetts	545.4	2,278.2				150.9	101.2	3,075.7
Michigan	401.9	1,248.4				216.7	99.1	1,966.0
Minnesota		343.8				80.4	1,179.1	1,603.3
Mississippi			14,602.0			140.0	26.2	14,768.2
Missouri		319.8				124.5	72.0	516.3
Montana	9.3	40.9	1,803.0		125.0	8.9	15.4	2,002.5
Nebraska	109.5	221.8				25.8	179.3	536.4
Nevada	262.5		179,667.1	2,257.3		15.0		182,202.0
New Hampshire	213.4	105.2				39.9	44.4	402.8
New Jersey	1,128.5	1,421.2	73,801.4			82.1	49.7	76,482.8
New Mexico	131.8					46.0	35.3	213.2
New York	2,853.8	2,373.7				176.1	90.8	5,494.4
North Carolina						69.1		69.1
North Dakota	7.1				274.1	56.1	236.6	573.8
Ohio	431.8	1,971.5				226.7	380.7	3,010.7
Oklahoma	214.1					65.4		279.5
Oregon	111.9	2,204.8			105.0	64.3	15.1	2,501.1
Pennsylvania	641.9	1,539.2				192.0		2,373.1
Rhode Island	141.1	339.5				17.0	15.8	513.4
South Carolina			1,638.8			84.0		1,722.8
South Dakota	9.9	1,728.7	510.7			14.1	13.3	2,276.7
Texas	509.9	2,265.9				506.4	152.9	3,435.1
Vermont	0.9	51.1				5.7	2.9	60.6
Virginia		842.7				64.5	157.9	1,065.1
Washington	160.2	328.8	396.0		289.4	194.7	122.5	1,491.5
West Virginia	249.9	185.8				18.1	9.0	462.8
Wisconsin	251.6	483.6				50.5	52.5	838.2
Wyoming	11.8					9.2	8.6	29.6
Totals	**$17,397.1**	**$30,872.6**	**$292,780.7**	**$2,257.3**	**$8,451.1**	**$4,226.1**	**$4,886.4**	**$360,871.2**

1 Does not include gaming on oceangoing cruise ships or on Indian Reservations.
2 Includes adjustments for potential underreporting in some States.

Columns may not add to totals due to rounding.

Source: *International Gaming & Wagering Business*, August 5, 1994

State and local governments needed money very badly. Many saw lotteries as an easy way to raise large amounts of money without upsetting the voters. Lottery promoters usually said that money earned from lotteries would be used for a good purpose, such as education or helping older people. During the 1980s, more and more states introduced lotteries, and, by the 1990s, about three-fourths of all states had lotteries.

TYPES OF LOTTERY GAMES

Instant Lottery

For $1, a player can buy a ticket and find out immediately if he or she has won something. The number is already printed on the ticket and is covered with a special coating. The person scratches off the coating to see if the hidden number or symbol is a "winning ticket." Every state that has a lottery has an instant lottery.

Numbers — or Pick 3, Pick 4

The player bets on a two- or three-digit number from 0 to 999. A winning number is then picked. Although the winner does not usually win a large amount of money, many people are winners. In 1993, 29 states, the District of Columbia, and Puerto Rico offered some type of numbers game.

Lotto

To play lotto, a bettor chooses any five to six numbers and bets between $1 and $4 on those numbers. Many hundreds of thousands, even millions, of people usually buy tickets for these lotteries, and so the jackpots can be huge — often many, many millions of dollars. Winning numbers are drawn every week. If no one wins, the money is added to the next week's drawing so the jackpot becomes even bigger.

Video Lottery

To play video lottery (called video lottery terminals or VLTs), the player puts a quarter or dollar bill in a video game and the machine prints out a ticket that can then be cashed in if it is a winner. VLTs have been successfully introduced in South Dakota, Montana, and West Virginia. Their success has led several other states to consider legalizing VLTs.

LOTTERY SALES

Lotteries are very big business. In 1986, lotteries surpassed casino gambling as the largest type of gambling business in America. According to *International Gaming & Wagering Business* magazine, Americans bet $30.9 billion on state and municipal lotteries in 1993, an increase of almost 21 percent over the total lottery sales for 1992 ($25.5 billion). (See Tables 5.1 and 5.2.) Industry gross revenues rose to a record $12.8 billion. The $1.38 billion, 12.1 percent revenue gain, secured for the industry a 37 percent share of the total 1993 U.S. market for commercial games.

Eugene Martin Christiansen (president of Christiansen/Cummings Associates, Inc., an independent consulting firm which surveys commercial gambling) writes a thorough report on the gaming business every year for *International Gaming & Wagering Business* magazine. Mr. Christiansen, in his 1994 report, gave credit to new lotteries for the overall increase in lottery sales even though sales in eight states dropped in 1993 (Figure 5.1). In 1993, Georgia was the newcomer to the lottery business with sales of $557.4 million. Texas ended its second year with a 116 percent increase over 1992 sales at $2.2 billion. Only Rhode Island and Oregon VLT sales reported greater increases. (Refer again to Table 5.2.)

LOTTERY PRIZES

The payoff to players from lotteries is much smaller than from other forms of gambling. Lotteries keep a much higher percentage of the money bet (41 percent) than any other type of gambling. For example, horse racing keeps 20 percent, the slot machines, 6 percent, casino tables, 2 percent, and bingo keeps 25 percent. Therefore, while lotteries account for only 7 to 8 percent of all monies bet, they bring

TABLE 5.2
State & Municipal Lottery Sales, 1993 Compared to 1992 (Calendar Years)

(In $ millions)

State	1992 Total Sales (Revised)	1993 Total Sales	Increase/(Decrease) Dollars	Percent
Video Lottery Terminals				
Oregon	$865.3	$1,920.3	$1,055.0	121.90%
Rhode Island1	50.8	217.4	166.5	327.60%
South Dakota2	1,498.0	1,695.2	197.1	13.20%
West Virginia	36.2	45.5	9.3	25.70%
Total VLTs	2,450.3	3,878.3	1,428.0	58.30%
All Other Games				
Arizona	259.7	284.1	24.4	9.40%
California	1,496.5	1,836.3	339.8	22.70%
Colorado	246.4	281.0	34.6	14.00%
Connecticut	568.9	507.0	(61.9)	-10.90%
Delaware	80.8	100.9	20.1	24.90%
District of Columbia	153.1	204.9	51.8	33.80%
Florida	2,058.1	2,297.2	239.2	11.60%
Georgia	0.0	557.4	557.4	N/A
Idaho	50.0	71.7	21.6	43.20%
Illinois	1,624.9	1,507.9	(117.0)	-7.20%
Indiana	425.1	567.1	142.0	33.40%
Iowa	182.3	218.0	35.7	19.60%
Kansas	86.8	141.0	54.2	62.40%
Kentucky	424.5	500.5	76.0	17.90%
Louisiana	494.3	401.7	(92.6)	-18.70%
Maine	119.7	130.6	10.8	9.10%
Maryland	822.0	970.8	148.8	18.10%
Massachusetts	1,866.4	2,278.2	411.8	22.10%
Michigan	1,250.6	1,248.4	(2.2)	-0.20%
Minnesota	320.5	343.8	23.3	7.30%
Missouri	223.3	319.8	96.5	43.20%
Montana	30.5	40.9	10.4	34.10%
Nebraska	112.3	221.8	109.5	97.50%
New Hampshire	107.2	105.2	(2.0)	-1.90%
New Jersey	1,352.9	1,421.2	68.3	5.00%
New York	2,270.3	2,373.7	103.5	4.60%
Ohio	1,844.5	1,971.5	126.9	6.90%
Oregon	253.8	284.5	30.7	12.10%
Pennsylvania	1,412.4	1,539.2	126.8	9.00%
Rhode Island	85.8	122.1	36.3	42.20%
South Dakota	21.6	33.5	11.9	55.00%
Texas	1,047.3	2,265.9	1,218.6	116.40%
Vermont	51.7	51.1	(0.6)	-1.10%
Virginia	851.9	842.7	(9.2)	-1.10%
Washington	339.1	328.8	(10.3)	-3.00%
West Virginia	86.5	140.4	53.8	62.20%
Wisconsin	476.2	483.6	7.4	1.60%
Total Other Games	$23,097.9	$26,994.3	$3,896.4	16.90%
Total Lottery Sales	25,548.2	30,872.6	5,324.4	20.80%

1 Total sales in Rhode Island (cash in plus credits played) estimated based on average payout of 90%.
2 Total sales in South Dakota (cash in plus credits played) estimated based on average payout of 91%
Note: In some states, data is for approximate calendar years based on weekly sales reports. Also, due to reporting differences from year to year, calendar year 1993 may not be strictly comparable to calendar year 1992 in some states. All figures are unaudited.

Columns may not add to totals due to rounding.

Source: *International Gaming & Wagering Business*, August 5, 1994

FIGURE 5.1

Percentage Change in Lottery Sales, 1992 - 1993

CHRISTIANSEN/CUMMINGS ASSOCIATES, INC.

Source: *International Gaming & Wagering Business*, August 5, 1994

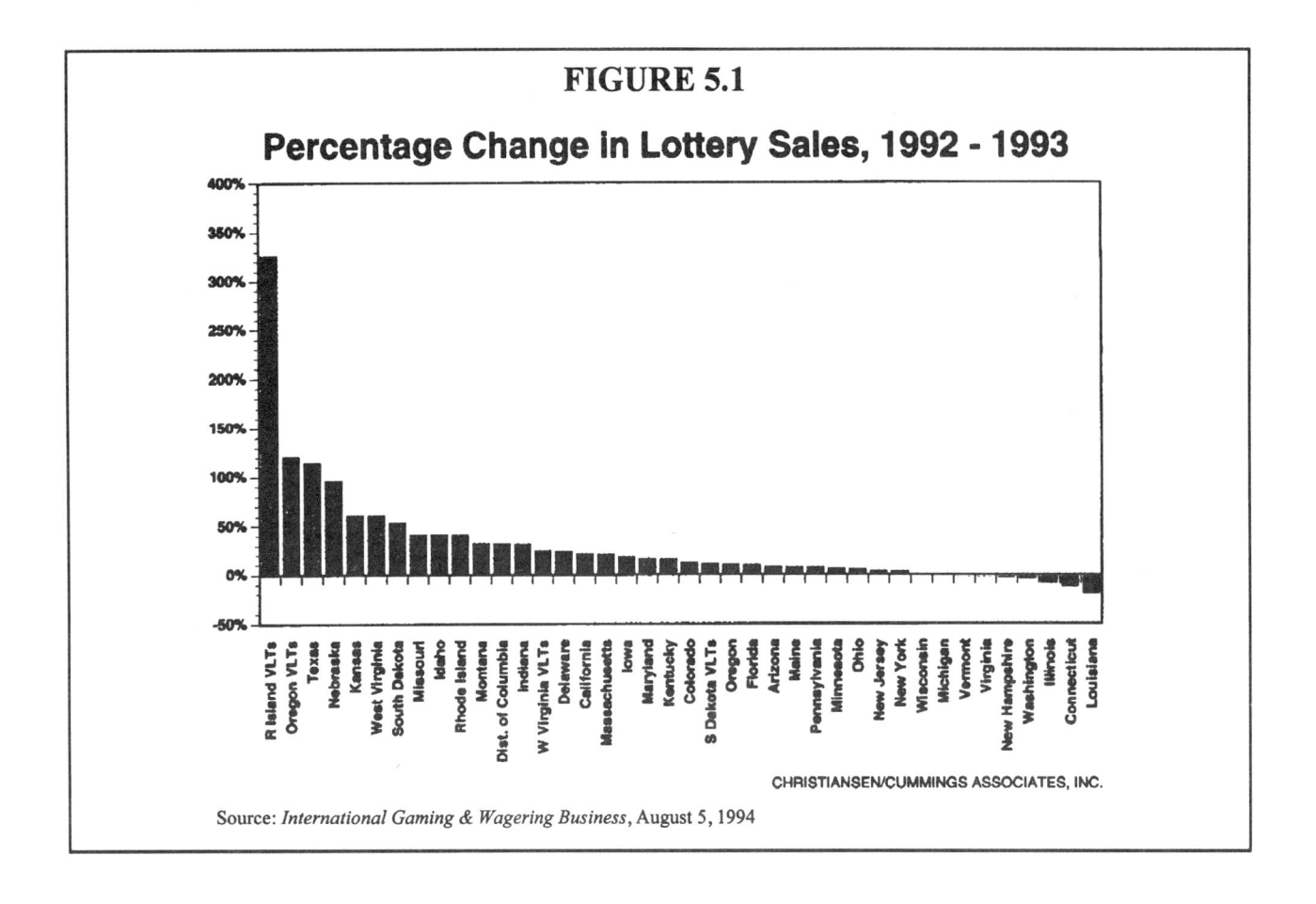

in 37 percent of all revenues (market share) because of the higher percentage the lotteries keep of the total monies bet. Figure 5.2 shows the percentages of total revenues (market share or money made) by each gaming activity in 1993.

Nonetheless, despite the fact that the chances of winning are very small, most Americans like to play the lottery. No skill is required, the tickets do not cost very much, and it is easy to buy a ticket. Lottery tickets may be sold in grocery stores, liquor stores, convenience stores, and newsstands. An estimated 6 billion tickets are sold every year in North America.

Because each ticket costs a dollar or maybe three or four, most people can afford to buy a ticket or two and feel they have not lost much money. Moreover, the prizes can be huge, often into the millions of dollars. Almost everyone dreams of winning millions of dollars and doing anything he or she would like to do.

HOW MUCH DOES THE GOVERNMENT GET IN TAXES?

One of the major arguments for lotteries is that they make money for the states and the money goes for good causes. New York, Michigan, New Hampshire, and California use their monies to fund education. New Jersey and Pennsylvania use their funds to help the elderly while Oregon builds school buildings and salmon highchairs (which help salmon get upstream to lay their eggs). Colorado uses its income from lotteries for parks and recreation, and Massachusetts gives the money to local governments and the arts. Arizona sets aside a special amount for transportation.

LOTTERIES THE WHOLE WORLD PLAYS

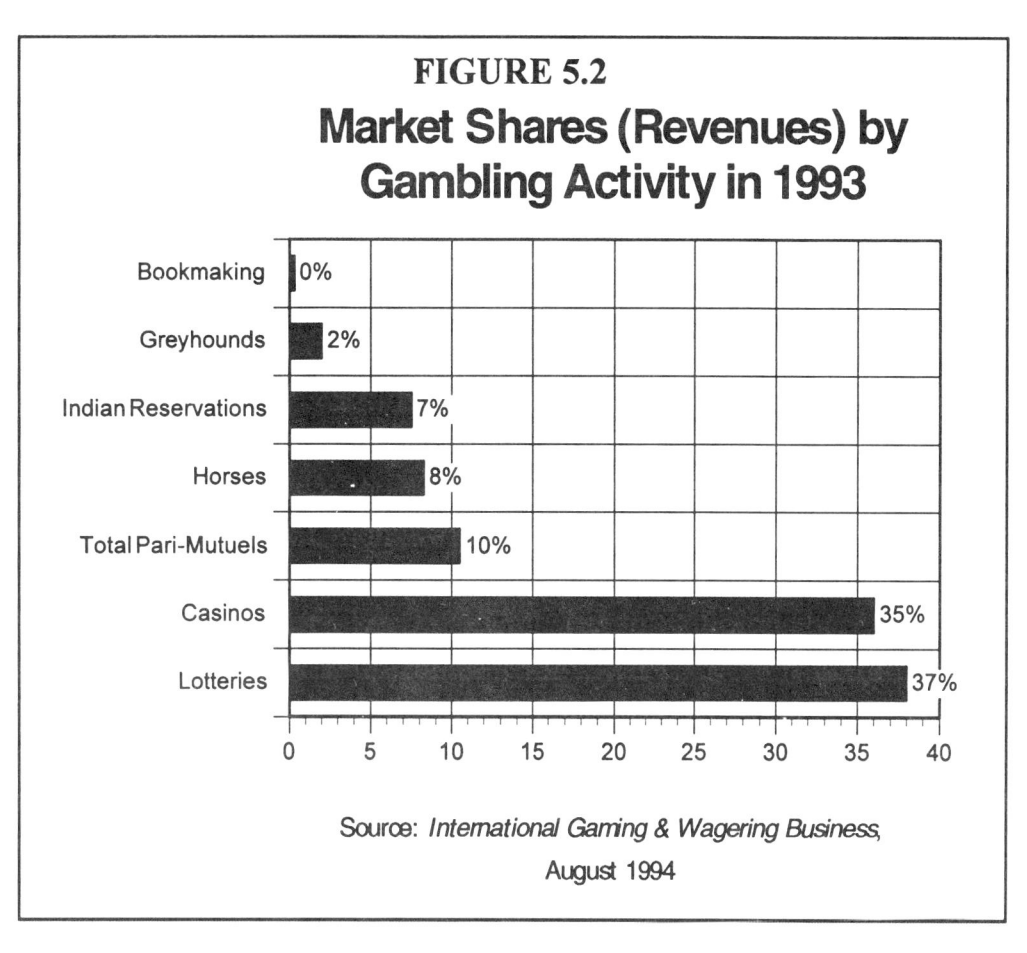

FIGURE 5.2
Market Shares (Revenues) by Gambling Activity in 1993

Activity	Percent
Bookmaking	0%
Greyhounds	2%
Indian Reservations	7%
Horses	8%
Total Pari-Mutuels	10%
Casinos	35%
Lotteries	37%

Source: *International Gaming & Wagering Business*, August 1994

Lotteries are as popular in other parts of the world as they are in the United States. Every continent has lotteries. According to *International Gaming & Wagering Business*, worldwide lottery sales (including the United States) reached $71.6 billion in 1991, up 11 percent from $64.4 billion in 1990. Europe had the most lottery sales ($29.7 billion), followed by North America ($25.5 billion), Asia ($8.7 billion), Australia and New Zealand ($2.3 billion), Central and South America ($1.4 billion), and Africa ($440 million). By country, the United States had the most lottery sales ($20.5 billion), followed by Spain ($7.2 billion), the Federal Republic of Germany ($7.2 billion), Japan ($5 billion), and Canada ($3.5 billion).

Electronic Future?

Lottery games are already on interactive home menus in France, Canada, and Japan; in September 1993, Switzerland's *Loterie Romande* introduced a videotext lottery using Swiss telephone lines. Belgium, France, Hungary, and Portugal are scheduled to participate in *Loterie Romande*. *International Gaming & Wagering Business* predicts that if this lottery succeeds in those countries, it could spread very rapidly throughout the rest of Europe and even the world.

CHAPTER VI

PUBLIC OPINION ABOUT GAMBLING

This chapter discusses two polls conducted by the Gallup Organization. The first, taken in 1992, is a nationwide sampling of American opinions on gambling activities in the United States. The second Gallup Poll, limited to New Jersey residents, was taken in 1993.

To find out how Americans felt about gambling, the Gallup Poll (Princeton, New Jersey) interviewed 1,208 adults 18 years and older in 1992. By that time, 35 states and the District of Columbia already had lotteries. These legal lotteries had made gambling easier for many Americans to accept. The Gallup researchers concluded that while gambling was growing in America, they also described a "cooling off" of enthusiasm for gambling. Rather than a loss of enthusiasm, this finding may mean that all the people who want to gamble are doing so, and those who do not probably will not.

TABLE 6.1

Opinion of Legal Gambling — Trend*

	Approve	Disapprove	No opinion
Bingo for cash prizes			
1992	72%	25%	3%
1989	75	23	2
1982	74	†	†
1975	68	†	†
Casino gambling at resort areas			
1992	51	47	2
1989	54	42	4
1982	51	†	†
1975	40	†	†
Casino gambling in a major city			
1992	40	57	3
Lotteries for cash prizes			
1992	75	24	1
1989	78	21	1
1982	72	†	†
1975	61	†	†
Offtrack betting on horse races			
1992	49	47	4
1989	54	42	4
1982	54	†	†
Betting on professional sports such as baseball, basketball, or football			
1992	33	65	2
1989	42	55	3
1982	51	†	†
1975	31	†	†
Casino gambling on Indian reservations			
1992	42	51	7
Casino gambling on so-called "river boats"			
1992	60	38	2

* 1975 data: University of Michigan
1982 data: Gallup for Gaming Business Magazine
† Data not available

Source: The Gallup Poll, Princeton, NJ, 1992

FIGURE 6.1

If additional states permit legalized betting on professional sports, do you think this would seriously affect the integrity and honesty of pro sports events, or not?

Affect Pro Sports' Integrity?

- No 31%
- Yes 64%
- No opinion 5%

Source: The Gallup Poll, Princeton, NJ, 1992

TABLE 6.2

Please tell me whether or not you have done any of the following things in the past 12 months. First, how about...

Gambling Activities — Trend
(Based on those responding "yes")

Played bingo for money
1992	9%
1989	13
1982*	9
1950	12

Visited a casino
1992	21%
1989	20
1984	18
1982*	12

Bet on a horse race
1992	12%
1989	14
1984	11
1982*	9
1950	4
1938	10

Bought a state lottery ticket
1992	56%
1989	54
1982*	18

Bet on a professional sports event such as baseball, basketball, or football
1992	12%
1989	22
1984	17
1982*	15

Bet on a *college* sports event such as basketball or football
1992	6%
1989	14

Bet on a boxing match
1992	6%
1989	8

Participated in an office pool on the World Series, Superbowl or other game
1992	22%

* Gallup for Gaming Magazine

Source: The Gallup Poll, Princeton, NJ, 1992

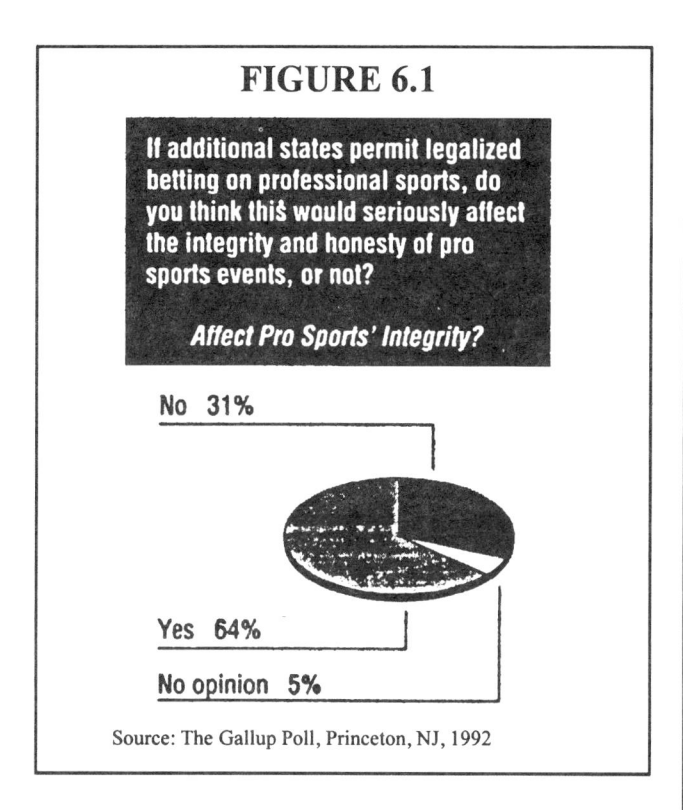

The Gallup researchers asked the people whether they approved or disapproved of various kinds of gambling. (See Table 6.1.) About 72 percent said they approved of bingo for cash prizes, down slightly from 75 percent in 1989. About half the country (51 percent) said that casino gambling in resort areas was all right, but only 40 percent approved of gambling in major cities such as New Orleans or Chicago. At the same time, 60 percent approved of casino gambling on riverboats. Even approval of lotteries had dropped somewhat from 78 percent in 1989 to 75 percent in 1992. Support for off-track betting on horses fell slightly from 54 percent in 1989 to 49 percent in 1992.

Americans did not feel comfortable about betting on professional sports such as baseball, basketball, and football. In 1982, 51 percent of those interviewed approved of it, but by 1992, only one-third (33 percent) of Americans thought betting on professional sports was a good idea. Almost two-thirds (64 percent) thought that allowing legal betting on professional sports would affect the honesty and outcome of the games (Figure 6.1).

HOW AMERICANS GAMBLE

The Gallup Poll found a significant decrease in how many Americans gambled in 1992 as compared to 1989. (See Table 6.2.) The proportion who played bingo within the past year fell from 13 percent in 1989 to 9 percent in 1992. Over the same period, the proportion of people who had bet on horse races dropped from 14 percent to 12 percent.

Betting on sporting events dropped sharply. The percentage betting on professional sports went from 22 percent in 1989 to only 12 percent in 1992. The proportion betting on college sports fell from 14 percent to 6 percent. Only casino betting (from 20 to 21 percent) and lottery tickets (from 54 to 56 percent) increased. The average amount spent monthly on lottery tickets fell from $53 in 1989 to $28 in 1992 (Table 6.3).

The fun has gone out of gambling for many Americans. While the proportion of people who enjoyed making bets "a lot" was the same (7 percent) in 1989 and 1992, the percentage of those who enjoyed gambling "a little" dropped from 27 percent to 22 percent. The proportion who did not like betting at all rose from 38 percent to 45 percent. (See Table 6.4.)

TABLE 6.3
How much money do you usually spend each month on lottery tickets? (based on those who purchased ticket in last 12 months)

Monthly Expenditures on Lottery — Trend

	1989	1992
$30 or more	12%	9%
$20-29	11	11
$10-19	18	19
$5-9	24	17
$1-4	22	28
Less than $1	11	14
No opinion	2	2
	100%	100%
Mean	$53	$28
Median	$5	$5

Source: The Gallup Poll, Princeton, NJ, 1992

DOES GAMBLING CAUSE TROUBLE?

The Gallup researchers asked, "Do you sometimes gamble more than you think you

TABLE 6.4
How much do you yourself enjoy making bets? Would you say you enjoy making bets a lot, a little, not too much or not at all?

Enjoy Gambling?

	1989	1992
A lot	7%	7%
A little	27	22
Not too	27	26
Not at all	38	45
No opinion	1	*
	100%	100%

* Less than 0.5%

Source: The Gallup Poll, Princeton, NJ, 1992

should?" About 9 percent (10 percent in 1989) thought they gambled too much (Table 6.5). When asked whether "gambling [has] ever been a source of problems in your family?" 5 percent answered that it had, about the same as the 4 percent in 1989 (Table 6.6).

THE COUNCIL ON COMPULSIVE GAMBLING OF NEW JERSEY SURVEY

The Council on Compulsive Gambling of New Jersey, Inc., notes that, for some people, gambling can cause very serious problems. The Council asked the Gallup Organization (Gallup Poll) of Princeton (NJ) to study "New Jersey residents' behavior and attitudes related to gambling." The results of the survey were based on telephone interviews with 1,016 adults 18 years and older in 1993.

The survey found that almost all New Jersey residents (96 percent) had gambled at some time during their lives. Most had played the lottery (82 percent), slot machines (75 percent), or gambled in a casino (74 percent). Half (50 percent) had bet on horse or dog racing and a significant percentage had played cards for money (44 percent), bingo for money (34 percent), and the numbers (31 percent). (See Table 6.7.) For a state with a lottery and a major gambling center in Atlantic City, these high percentages should not be surprising.

Among those who gambled, 40 percent played the lottery at least once a week, 31 percent played the numbers at least once a week, 19 percent bowled, shot pool, or played golf for money at least once a week, and 11 percent played cards for money at least once a week. When asked about the largest amount of money they had ever gambled, most (53 percent) had never gambled more than $100. The average largest amount was $403 and only about 8 percent had ever gambled $1,000 or more at one time. (See Table 6.8.)

Getting Hooked

When asked how often they went back to win the money they had lost, 80 percent

---

TABLE 6.5

Do you sometimes gamble more than you think you should?
NEW JERSEY
Gamble Too Much? — Trend

	1989	1992
Yes	10%	9%
No	90	91
	•	•
	100%	100%

• Less than 0.5%

Source: The Gallup Poll, Princeton, NJ, 1993

TABLE 6.6

Has gambling ever been a source of problems within your family?
NEW JERSEY
Gambling Caused Family Problems? — Trend

	1989	1992
Yes	4%	5%
No	96	95
No opinion	•	1
	100%	100%

• Less than 0.5%

Source: The Gallup Poll, Princeton, NJ, 1993

said that they never did. However, 16 percent said they did some of the time, 3 percent, most of the time, and 1 percent, every time. When asked, "Have you ever gambled more than you intended?" 77 percent said no and 23 percent said yes. Men (28 percent) were more likely to have gambled more than they intended than women (18 percent). Younger people were more likely to gamble more than they intended than were older people.

About 5 percent said they would like to stop gambling but could not. Eight percent of men and 2 percent of women would have liked to stop gambling but could not. About 3 percent of those interviewed saw gambling as a way to escape their problems.

Do You Know a Problem Gambler?

Three-quarters (76 percent) said that they did not know anyone with a gambling problem; 14 percent knew a friend; 13 percent knew a relative; 3 percent had fathers who had trouble with gambling; and 2 percent had spouses with problems. (See Table 6.9.) About 4 percent said that gambling, either by the person asked or a member of the family, had made his or her home life unhappy. Twenty-eight percent said they knew someone who gambled too much but did not necessarily have a gambling problem.

TABLE 6.7

TYPES OF GAMBLING EVER DONE

	Total %	Gender Male %	Female %	Age 18-34 %	35-49 %	50-64 %	65+ %
Played the lottery	82	85	80	82	88	84	70
Played slot machines, poker machines or other gambling machines	75	79	72	72	81	78	72
Gambled in a casino (legal or otherwise)	74	79	70	67	82	81	69
Bet on horses, dogs or other animals (at OTB, the track or with a bookie)	50	57	43	44	55	58	43
Played cards for money	44	59	31	48	46	42	37
Played bingo for money	34	28	40	25	39	37	39
Played the numbers	31	35	28	30	32	28	35
Played scratch off games other than lotteries	31	34	28	38	27	30	23
Bet on sports (parlay cards, with a bookie, or at Jai Alai)	26	41	13	34	26	24	13
Bowled, shot pool, played golf or some other game of skill for money	25	38	12	32	22	25	12
Played the stock, options and/or commodities market	24	30	20	21	29	30	17
Played dice games (including craps, over and under or other dice games) for money	19	30	8	20	18	20	15

Source: *New Jersey Residents' Attitudes and Behavior Regarding Gambling*, prepared by the Gallup Organization, Inc., for The Council on Compulsive Gambling of New Jersey, Inc. (Princeton, NJ, 1993)

Who Should Help Compulsive Gamblers?

Most people in the New Jersey poll believed that the state and the legal gambling companies should help treat compulsive gamblers and contribute to educate people living in the state about gambling. A large majority (78 percent) thought the state should educate students about gambling while 58 percent believed the state should pay for treating compulsive gamblers. Almost three-fourths (72 percent) agreed that gambling companies should provide financial support for gambling programs.

Where Do You Go for Help?

The Gallup researchers asked if the New Jerseyites knew where to get help for gambling problems and addiction. About half (48 percent) said they knew where to go for help and half (52 percent) did not. Among those who did not know where to go, 38 percent mentioned Gamblers Anonymous, and another 18 percent said they would look in the phone book. Only about 12 percent knew to call 1-800-GAMBLER, the helpline set up by the Council on Compulsive Gambling of New Jersey, Inc., to help those addicted to gambling.

ATTITUDES ABOUT GAMBLING

Most people believed that gambling just naturally poses some risks to society, but only 22 percent believed that gambling is immoral. Those over age 65 (30 percent)

TABLE 6.8
LARGEST AMOUNT EVER GAMBLED

	Total %	Men %	Women %
Under $10	14	11	17
$10-49	26	20	32
$50-99	13	12	13
$100-149	15	15	16
$150-199	1	2	1
$200-249	8	11	5
$250-299	*	*	*
$300-399	3	3	2
$400-499	2	2	1
$500-599	4	6	3
$600-999	1	1	*
$1,000 or more	8	13	4
Don't know	5	4	6
Total	100	100	100
MEAN	$403	$594	$219
Number of Interviews	(976)	(504)	(472)

*Less than one-half of one percent.

Source: *New Jersey Residents' Attitudes and Behavior Regarding Gambling*, prepared by the Gallup Organization, Inc., for The Council on Compulsive Gambling of New Jersey, Inc. (Princeton, NJ, 1993)

and those earning less than $25,000 a year were most likely to believe gambling is wrong.

Sixty-six percent thought that gambling "encourage[d] people who can least afford to spend money gambling," and 57 percent agreed that legal gambling can make compulsive gamblers out of people who would never gamble if it were against the law. Sixty-one percent thought it "opened the door" for organized crime, and 59 percent thought that gambling can wear away young people's ideals about the value of work. They were divided about half and half about the statement that gambling teaches children that one can get something for nothing: 49 percent agreed and 48 percent disagreed.

WHY DO PEOPLE GAMBLE?

The Gallup researchers asked, "what is the main reason you like to gamble?" Most people (39 percent) gambled because they wanted to have a good time or for recreation or fun, although many (27 percent) gambled to make money or get rich. Twelve percent played for the excitement and another 11 percent saw it as a challenge. Most people gamble for some type of recreation, enjoyment, excitement, or fun.

TABLE 6.9

PEOPLE IN LIFE WHO HAVE GAMBLING PROBLEM

	Total %	Gender Male %	Female %
Relative (NET)	13	12	14
Spouse	2	*	3
Father	3	3	3
Mother	1	1	1
Brother or sister	2	2	2
Children	*	*	*
Another relative	7	6	7
A friend	14	17	10
No one	76	74	78
Don't know/Refused	*	*	*
Number of Interviews	(1016)	(515)	(501)

*Less than one-half of one percent.

Source: *New Jersey Residents' Attitudes and Behavior Regarding Gambling*, prepared by the Gallup Organization, Inc., for The Council on Compulsive Gambling of New Jersey, Inc. (Princeton, NJ, 1993)

CHAPTER VII

THE DEBATE OVER THE LOTTERY*

THE LOTTERY IS A GOOD IDEA

PREPARED STATEMENT BY DR. MARCIA LYNN WHICKER, PROFESSOR OF PUBLIC ADMINISTRATION, AND DR TODD W. ARESON, ASSISTANT DIRECTOR OF CENTER FOR PUBLIC AFFAIRS, SCHOOL OF COMMUNITY AND PUBLIC AFFAIRS, VIRGINIA COMMONWEALTH UNIVERSITY, DECEMBER 10, 1987.

Marcia Whicker and Todd Areson are both from Virginia Commonwealth University. However, the opinions they give are their own and not the opinion of Virginia Commonwealth University. While they present both sides of the argument over the lottery, they generally give more weight to the side supporting the lottery. Furthermore, they believe the time has come for the lottery.

---

*The opinions have been selected from testimony before U.S. Congressional committees or from debates that took place on the floor of Congress. Some words may be difficult to understand. If the editors have replaced one word with another, that word is enclosed in brackets []. If the editors feel it is important to know the word, the word will be followed by another word in italics explaining it. This word is enclosed in parentheses ().

Two very important words mentioned throughout this debate — regressive and compulsive. In this case, regressive refers to taxation. A regressive tax is a tax in which poor people pay a higher percentage of their income than rich people. For example, the sales tax is a regressive tax. If a loaf of bread costs a dollar and the tax is ten cents, both the rich person and the poor person pay ten cents. The ten cents is a larger percentage of the poor person's income than it is of the rich person's income.

Compulsive, in this case, refers to compulsive gamblers. These are people who cannot stop gambling. Just as drinking can destroy an alcoholic's life, so gambling can destroy a compulsive gambler's life. They may lose their families money and go deep into debt. Gamblers Anonymous is designed to help compulsive gamblers stop their gambling, just as Alcoholics Anonymous is meant to help alcoholics stop drinking. (See Chapter I.)

LOTTERIES AS A METHOD OF RAISING GOVERNMENT REVENUES

While the lottery is pushed by supporters as a method of raising revenues for government without raising taxes, how lucrative is it? Where they exist, lotteries amount for only a small percentage of state funding, typically two to four percent. Yet even a small percent can lead to substantial dollar amounts in larger states.

Lotteries have several pros and cons. Typically they are opposed by religious groups, which contend gambling is sinful. Supporters counter that churches themselves use "ungodly" gambling in the forms of bingo and raffles to raise revenues.

Critics argue that state lotteries encourage gambling and feed gambling addictions. Supporters argue that Americans are going to gamble anyway, and do so in the form of office pools, betting on professional football and basketball games, and illegal numbers games. Better, they say, that gambling proceeds be used to support desirable public purposes, such as education, medical care for the indigent (poor people), or services for the elderly than to serve illegal ends.

Supporters counter that comparing the lottery to taxes is unfair since it is not a tax. When viewed as a service, and compared to the costs of producing other types of entertainment, the yield for lotteries is high. The question of [giving] lottery revenues for special purposes is also controversial. While tying lottery proceeds to popular causes makes lottery adoption more politically [acceptable], critics contend that it hamstrings (makes more difficult) future budget decisions in the legislature and may result in funds being spent for purposes after the need has disappeared.

Perhaps the greatest criticism of the lottery, however, is that it is regressive, placing the greatest burden upon the poor, who buy more lottery tickets than the middle class or the rich. A 1975 study of the Connecticut, Massachusetts, and Pennsylvania lotteries examined the annual expenditure per family in those states. While the average expenditure in absolute dollars was greatest for middle income families, expenditures, as a percent of family income, were greater for low income families. This supports the notion that the impact of lotteries is regressive. [Supporters], however, maintain that the lottery must be evaluated against the regressivity of its alternatives. Other types of ... taxes, especially the general sales tax, are equally regressive. Furthermore, a 1983 study of the Washington state lottery found that playing games there was growing in popularity with middle income citizens.

Despite its disadvantages, governments ... have found lotteries an acceptable method of raising revenue. While states run government-sponsored lotteries in the U.S., Britain conducts national lotteries. There, horse racing and bingo are two popular forms of lotteries. With recent mandates (requirements) to government to do more with less and increasing pressure on politicians not to raise taxes, nationwide, the lottery is an idea that just won't go away.

TESTIMONY OF MARTIN M. PUNCKE, DIRECTOR MARYLAND STATE LOTTERY, AND PRESIDENT NORTH-AMERICAN ASSOCIATION OF STATE LOTTERIES BEFORE THE COMMITTEE ON GOVERNMENTAL AFFAIRS, UNITED STATES SENATE, OCTOBER 3, 1984.

Martin Puncke is Director of the Maryland State Lottery and president of the North American Association of State Lotteries, the industry organization that promotes state lotteries. Mr. Puncke does not believe that lotteries are regressive and he thinks that lotteries are a form of recreation that people voluntarily choose to play.

I believe a legal lottery is an appropriate (proper) function of State government.... I further believe that this type of revenue (money) has proven to be a dependable revenue source and should be allowed to operate by the State without [interference] by any other level of government. States should have the primary responsibility for determining what forms of gambling may legally take place within their boundaries.

A regressive tax is a tax which is applied to the entire population equally regardless of the financial status of any individual, thereby taking a larger percentage of the income from a low income group in proportion to a higher income group. Several studies ... clearly and consistently verify the fact that lower income persons do not play the lottery in a greater proportion than their income group is in proportion to the general population.

No one is required to play the lottery; it is strictly voluntary. It is a consumer product which competes in the free marketplace, and has prospered and grown.... We are all aware that the most regressive form of taxation is the sales tax because it is levied (required) without regard for an individual income level and the poor pay a disproportionate amount of their income toward such a tax. A tax is compulsory while [a person can choose whether or not to] purchase of a lottery ticket...

TESTIMONY OF DANIEL W. BOWER, PRESIDENT, SCIENTIFIC GAMES, INC., BEFORE THE COMMITTEE ON GOVERNMENTAL AFFAIRS, UNITED STATES SENATE, OCTOBER 3, 1984.

Daniel Bower is president of Scientific Games, Inc., a company that produces gambling machines. He believes lotteries have produced a lot of money for state governments. He does not believe that the lottery is a regressive tax but a voluntary choice. Mr. Bower sees no connection between lotteries and crime, nor does he feel that lotteries are a danger to compulsive gamblers.

Probably the most dominant question asked about a lottery is how much revenue it can raise for a state.... It is amazing to realize that gross revenues from United

States lotteries have increased from $40 million in 1970 to over $6 billion in 1983!

Myths about a state lottery.

a. Lotteries and the poor.

Perhaps the most repeated objection to state operated lotteries is that poor people buy a disproportionate amount of lottery tickets. Some people take offense at objections to lotteries on this ground because, as Mayor Ernest Morial of New Orleans once said, "[I find it distasteful that some people are telling other people how they should run their own lives.] In any event, the attack is totally [without truth]. Numerous ... studies have been done about the [people who play the lottery]. These studies establish that lower income people play the lottery to a lesser degree than their proportion of the population. Typically, most lottery tickets are bought by persons between the ages of 35 and 54 whose household incomes are between $12,000 and $36,000. A related argument is that lotteries are a "regressive tax." However, a lottery is not a tax. It is an entirely voluntary activity on which people spend their discretionary (extra) income.

b. Lotteries and crime.

An objection that occasionally emerges is that lotteries create a law enforcement problem. Perhaps this objection finds its origin in the lottery scandals of the early 1800s when lotteries were operated by private companies. Or, perhaps this objection finds its origin in prejudices about lotteries based on [what people think] occur in the privately operated gaming industries of horse racing and casinos. Whatever the source of the objection, the objection itself is totally unfounded. Twenty years of experience with modern state lotteries has established conclusively that lotteries do not encourage crime and, in fact, quite the reverse is probably true.

c. Compulsive gambling.

Occasionally, certain individuals associated with the treatment of compulsive gambling allege that lotteries create compulsive gamblers. These same people argue that a portion of the revenues from the sale of lottery tickets should be spent on compulsive gambling treatment centers. However, there is no factual basis to this claim. Even Monsignor Joseph Dunn, the President of the National Council on Compulsive Gambling, admits that there is "no acceptable research" done to establish that state operated lotteries cause compulsive gambling. In fact, a study by the Colorado State Lottery concluded that "lottery games, in general, do not appeal to persons whose compulsive behavior evidences itself in gambling or risk taking on a compulsive basis."

THE LOTTERY IS A BAD IDEA

TESTIMONY OF GERARD FULCHER ON BEHALF OF THE DELAWARE STATE GAMING COMMISSION BEFORE THE SENATE COMMITTEE ON GOVERNMENTAL AFFAIRS, OCTOBER 3, 1984.

Gerald Fulcher is a member of the Delaware State Gaming Commission. He believes that gambling leads to crime and creates new gamblers.

Let's talk about profits, let's talk about what they call profits. They will tell you to measure the amount taken in, subtract the money you give to win, and subtract the overhead, subtract the money you give back to agents for being the middle man in this operation, and that is what they would like to label as profit.

But you have got to do a lot more subtracting. If they want to consider this as a business, then you subtract all the costs related to that business. That means you have to subtract the dollars and cents cost of criminal activity directly related to lotteries.... Lotteries do not raise terrific amounts of money when you subtract all of the costs involved. In order to perpetuate (keep it going) their bureaucracy, they have had to create a new [group] of gamblers to partake in their [business] on a regular basis. The State has literally had to create new gamblers. Our study shows that 12 percent of the people who play the lottery regularly, and we estimate regularly to be three or more times a week, (12 percent of them) virtually never gambled before it was legalized. So one of their basic [claims], that they are just giving the people already gambling an opportunity to do it legally, is a false [claim].

TESTIMONY OF DR. LARRY BRAIDFOOT, GENERAL COUNSEL, THE CHRISTIAN LIFE COMMISSION, SOUTHERN BAPTIST CONVENTION, NASHVILLE, TENNESSEE, EXCERPTED FROM THE PAMPHLET, "STATE OPERATED LOTTERIES."

Larry Braidfoot is a lawyer for the Christian Life Commission. He thinks gambling is a regressive tax on the poor, but what is more important, he believes gambling is immoral. It is immoral to take money from the poor who cannot afford it. Gambling makes government irresponsible, thinking it can solve all its problems by raising money from gambling. It is immoral when the government puts ads on television encouraging people to gamble.

The current drive to legalize state-operated lotteries has grown out of the increasing demands upon state budgets. State legislatures are looking for funds to meet the budget crises of the 1980s. Increasing taxes is never a popular thing for lawmakers to do.

Those who favor legalizing state lotteries usually present the following argument. The state needs more money. Increasing taxes is not popular; therefore, it is wise to consider some form of "taxation" which is voluntary. People are going to gamble, the argument continues. So it makes sense to legalize the gambling and to get some needed revenue (money) for the states. This will have the additional benefit of pulling money away from illegal gambling which produces revenue (money) for organized crime.

WHAT A LEGALIZED LOTTERY WILL REALLY DO?

State-operated lotteries appeal dramatically to the poorest citizens of the state. There can be no reasonable doubt that the daily numbers game, the one upon which most of the state operated lotteries depend for their main source of revenue (money), appeals primarily (mainly) to the poor and to the minority members of our society. Its appeal is based on the illusory (not real) promise and the desperate hope of a big win.

Daniel W. Bower is president and co-founder of Scientific Games, a corporation which specializes in lottery products and services. According to Bower, the "player selection" or numbers game attracts low-income minority players.... There can be no doubt, ... that the most popular and lucrative (money-making) lottery game is both targeted at and draws primarily from poor people.

Mark Abrahamson, a sociology professor at the University of Connecticut, reported to Connecticut's gaming commission that its daily lottery "primarily attracts poor, long term unemployed and less educated [lottery players]." Daniel B. Suits, an economics professor at Michigan State University, has pointed out on several occasions that low-income lottery players wager a [more than normal or ordinary] high percentage of their income on the lottery.... Perhaps the most conclusive evidence of the manner in which lotteries appeal to poor people is the fact that their outlets are concentrated (centered) in poorer neighborhoods. One... study was done in New Castle County, Delaware, in 1979. The study found no lottery outlets in the upper-income neighborhoods where 17,630 persons lived. There was one lottery outlet for every 17,774 persons in upper-middle income neighborhoods. There was one lottery outlet for every 5,032 persons in the lower-middle to middle-income neighborhoods. There was one lottery outlet for every 1,981 persons in the poorest neighborhoods.

STATE-OPERATED LOTTERIES ARE A REGRESSIVE AND INEFFICIENT WAY TO RAISE TAXES

A form of taxation is regressive if it draws a larger percentage of its revenue from the poorer citizens than from middle- and upper-class citizens. It is regressive if a poorer person spends a higher percentage of his or her income on the activity than does the person of modest or affluent means. Such is clearly the case with the lottery.

STATES WHICH SEEK TO RESOLVE THEIR FISCAL WOES BY LEGALIZING GAMBLING ACHIEVE MINIMAL SUCCESS

Revenues from gambling amount to little more than a patch on a state's financial woes (problems).... Once states begin turning to legalized gambling for a source of revenue (money), the temptation builds to fix other financial woes by legalizing additional forms of gambling. Rather than bringing fiscal responsibility, the tendency is established to seek easy solutions to difficult financial problems. Most legalized gambling ventures (programs) generate much less than the amounts [estimated] prior to legalization.

STATE-OPERATED LOTTERIES DO NOT SUCCESSFULLY ELIMINATE OR REDUCE ILLEGAL GAMBLING.

Lottery advocates [argue] that the legalization of lotteries will persuade many individuals who currently bet in illegal games to switch to the legal game. Whether or not some of the players actually switch is uncertain. What is clear, however, is that there is no significant decrease in illegal gambling and illegal numbers games flourish alongside legal lotteries. Legal lotteries do not compete very well with the illegal games.

LEGALIZING GAMBLING IS A MORAL ISSUE

The decision to legalize gambling is a moral issue:

Pro-gambling forces advocate [want] a morality which essentially justifies the gambling (the means) by the revenue it produces (the end). This is one type of morality. Another type ... is a materialistic morality which longs for the opportunity of getting something for nothing, for the chance of being able to "get rich quick" apart from labor or the creation of a product of real value.

It is a moral issue when the state decides to derive income from an activity which is a regressive form of taxation that affects poor people more than affluent [well-to-do] people. It is a moral issue when a state decides not only to tolerate gambling but to get in the business of planning games, engaging in promotional activities (radio, television, newspapers, billboards), and targeting its citizens through extensive marketing analyses in the hopes of creating new gamblers to contribute taxes through an inefficient form of "tax farming."

It is a moral issue when a state adopts a form of gambling which in all probability will increase the extent and the amount of illegal gambling. It is a moral issue when a state adopts a form of gambling that will draw off large amounts of money especially from the poor people for whom the state supposedly has a responsibility to provide assistance.

PREPARED STATEMENT OF STATE REPRESENTATIVE JERRY KOPEL (CO) DECEMBER 23, 1987.

Jerry Kopel is a state representative from Colorado. He thinks it is wrong that the state puts ads on television encouraging people to dream of getting rich quick. He furthermore sees it as a tax that takes money from the people and gives it to the government.

Often players become bored with "numbers"... the next game will likely be cable-TV play at-home, or electronic poker, with no skill involved.... Big jackpots will always get bigger, and states will merge games across the borders.... Some other business will always lose the dollar that is diverted to lottery; someone doesn't buy a straw hat, or a necktie, or go to a movie.

Lottery is a state monopoly, and the state uses its gaming proceeds to urge residents to place their bets, stressing the pleasures gained from winning, and down-playing the horrendous odds of winning. The advertising appeal is answered by those who often dream of getting rich, the ones who have the least money. Studies ... show that the poor spend more of their net income for lottery than do any other group. And the state creates new gamblers where none existed, especially when the game duplicates the illegal numbers game.

Lottery [supporters] don't like to hear the lottery called a tax, but most impartial [do not take sides for or against] economists recognize it as such because of the transfer (moving) of income from an individual to the state. As a way of financing government, it is the least efficient with extremely high overhead costs compared to other tax collections. If history is any guide, the lottery is a fad that will eventually fade. States that don't adopt one will end up healthier for not doing so.

GLOSSARY

casino — a building or a room where gambling, such as slot machines and table games (blackjack, roulette, etc.) takes place.

fix — when someone, usually a gambler, pays a player in a sporting event to change the outcome of the event. A boxer may be paid to lose a boxing match. A basketball player may be paid to score fewer points than he or she normally could.

gaming — another word for gambling.

handle — the total amount of money bet by all bettors on a gambling activity. The daily handle at the racetrack is the total amount of money bet that day.

harness racing — form of horse racing in which the rider sits in a carriage, or sulky, and directs the horse around the track. A harness racing horse may be either a trotter or a pacer.

jai-alai — a very fast game in which the players use a large, curved basket strapped to the arm to catch and whip a small, hard ball against three walls and the floor of a huge playing court in much the same way as handball or racquetball are played. Originating among the Basque people in the western Pyrenees mountains, jai-alia means "merry festival."

lottery — a game in which players buy a numbered ticket and hope to win a prize if their number is the one drawn from among all of those who have bought tickets for the lottery.

off-track betting (OTB) — a bettor may bet on a horse or dog race without being at the racetrack. OTB bets are usually placed at a track branch office or a betting shop or parlor.

pacer — a horse used in harness racing. A pacer moves both left legs forward at the same time, then both right legs.

pari-mutuel — a type of betting in which bettors wager against each other. The money wagered is put into a pool and then split among the winners.

pay-off — the amount of money gotten from the bets which is left after the take-out. This amount is given back to the winning bettors.

place — in a horse or dog race, the horse or dog that comes in second.

quarter horse — a very swift horse that can run faster than other horses for a short distance. The name refers to the quarter-mile race the horse runs.

riverboat — traditionally, a large paddle-wheel boat that sails up and down the Mississippi, Missouri, and Ohio Rivers. During the nineteenth century these boats were used for moving freight and passengers. Now they are used for entertainment as floating restaurants, cruise ships, and gambling ships.

show — in a horse or dog race, the horse or dog that comes in third.

simulcast — the racetrack shows the race live on television at another racetrack or at a gambling parlor or at a simulcasting theater where the race is shown on a big screen at the same time the race is happening. People then can bet on the race just as if they were at the racetrack.

table games — those gambling games that are normally played on a table. They include poker, roulette, craps, and blackjack.

take-out — the percentage of the amount of the handle that is taken out by the person or company that runs the gambling activity and the state government, mostly in the form of taxes.

thoroughbred — a racing horse with a heritage approved and registered by the New York Jockey Club. Thoroughbreds run with the rider seated in a saddle mounted directly on the horse's back.

trotter — a horse used in harness racing. A trotter moves the left front and right rear legs forward almost at the same time, then moves the right front and left rear legs.

wager — to make a bet. To "put down" money on a gambling activity: *The man wagered (bet) $10 on the horse to win.* Also, the amount of the bet: *The wager on the boxing match was $100.*

win — in a horse or dog race, the horse or dog that comes in first.

IMPORTANT NAMES AND ADDRESSES

American Greyhound Track Operators Association
1065 NE 125 St.
Suite 219
North Miami, FL 33161-5832
(305) 893-2101
FAX (305) 893-5633

American Quarter Horse Association
1600 Quarter Horse Drive
Amarillo, TX 79168
(806) 376-4811
FAX (806) 376-8364

Association of Racing Commissioners
International, Inc.
2343 Alexandria Dr., Suite 200
Lexington, KY 40504
(606) 224-7070
FAX (606) 224-7071

Colorado Division of Gaming
720 South Colorado Blvd.
Denver, CO 80222
(303) 757-7555
FAX (303) 757-8624

Compulsive Gambling Center, Inc.
924 East Baltimore St.
Baltimore, MD 21202-4739
(800) 332-0402

Council on Compulsive Gambling
of New Jersey, Inc.
1315 West State St.
Trenton, NJ 08618
(609) 599-3299
1-800-GAMBLER
FAX (609) 599-9383

Gamblers Anonymous
International Service Office
P.O. Box 17173
Los Angeles, CA 90017
(213) 386-8789

Gaming and Wagering Business
BMT Publications
Seven Penn Plaza
New York, NY 10001-3900
(212) 594-4120
FAX (212) 714-0514

Harness Tracks of America
22 Pea Pack Road
P.O. Box 931
Far Hills, NJ 07931
(908) 234-9300
FAX (908) 234-1702

National Association of Fundraising
Ticket Manufacturers
P.O. Box 2385
Bismarck, ND 58502
(701) 223-1660
FAX (701) 255-6325

National Indian Gaming Association
904 Pennsylvania SE
Washington, DC 20003
(202) 546-7711
FAX (202) 546-1755

National Indian Gaming Commission
1850 M St. NW
Suite 250
Washington, DC 20036
(202) 632-7003
FAX (202) 632-7066

North American Association
of State and Provincial Lotteries
1726 M St. NW
Washington, DC 20036
(202) 223-2423
FAX (202) 833-1577

U.S. Trotting Association
750 Michigan Ave.
Columbus, Oh 43215
(614) 224-2291
FAX (614) 224-4575

State of South Dakota
Commission on Gaming
118 East Missouri
Pierre, SD 57501-5070
(605) 773-6050
FAX (605) 773-6053

RESOURCES

Gambling in America (WDC, 1976), the final report of the Commission on the Review of the National Policy Toward Gambling, despite its age, continues to be the most complete government study on the subject. The Commission asked the Survey Research Center of the University of Michigan to do a very large and detailed study of gambling. With few exceptions, the Commission accepted the results of that study.

Gaming and Wagering Business, a monthly magazine devoted to the gaming industry, contains valuable information on every aspect of the industry and regularly publishes special reports on particular types of gambling activity such as lotteries and casino gambling. Information Plus continues to extend its sincere appreciation to the magazine for permission to use material from its publications.

The Association of Racing Commissioners International (Lexington, KY) publishes an annual report, *PariMutuel Racing*, that summarizes statistics on horse racing, greyhound racing, and jai alai events. Information Plus thanks the Association for permission to use material from their publication.

The American Greyhound Track Operators Association (North Miami, FL) every year publishes *Track Facts* and the *Summary of State Pari-Mutuel Tax Structures* which concentrates on state taxing, revenue, and greyhound racing. The *Official Handbook of the American Quarter Horse Association* provides an overview of quarter horse racing in America.

The states of Nevada and New Jersey each publish a detailed yearly report on casino gambling. The *Nevada Gaming Abstract* is put out by the State Gaming Control Board (Carson City, NV) while the New Jersey Casino Control Commission (Trenton, NJ) issues an *Annual Report*. Both publications provide complete statistical information on casino gambling in those states. Other states in which casino gambling is legal, such as Colorado and South Dakota also publish reports.

The Federal Bureau of Investigation maintains statistics on gambling arrests in its annual *Uniform Crime Reports — Crime in the United States*. As always, Information Plus expresses its sincere appreciation to the Gallup Poll (Princeton, NJ) and the National Opinion Research Center at the University of Chicago (IL) and the Roper Center for Public Opinion Research at the University of Connecticut for permission to use material from their surveys.

Information Plus would like to thank the Excalibur Hotel in Las Vegas, NV for permission to use the photograph of their hotel. Information Plus also thanks The Council on Compulsive Gambling of New Jersey, Inc., and Executive Director Arnie Wexler for permission to use material from the survey, *New Jersey Residents' Attitudes and Behavior Regarding Gambling*, prepared by the Gallup Organization, Inc., and for other materials prepared by the Council and Mr. Wexler.

INDEX

Atlantic City, 23-25
Betting, 12ff
    off-track, 16, 17, 19
    pari-mutuel, 12ff
    simulcasting, 16, 17, 19
Bingo, 5
"Black Sox" scandal, 3
Bower, Daniel W., testimony of, 43-44
Braidford, Dr. Larry, testimony of, 45-48
British Stamp Act, 2
Canadian gaming, 8
Casinos, 10-27
    card rooms, 21, 26-27
    Native American, 10, 22
    Nevada, 20-21, 23
    New Jersey, 21, 24
    riverboat gambling, 25-26
    slot machines, 22
    table games, 22
Cruises, 26
Dog racing, 17-18
    coursing, 17
    greyhound, 17-18
    Sport of Queens, 17
Franklin, Benjamin, 2
Fulcher, Gerard, testimony of, 45
Gambling, 5ff
    compulsive, 37-39, 40, 44, *See* also Gamblers Anonymous
    definitions, 5
    illegal, 9
    Indian reservations, 4, 10-11
    laws, 6, 14
    public opinion about, 34-36
    types of legal, 5-6
Gambling house, 2, *See* also Casino
Gamblers Anonymous, 4, 39
Gaming, 5, *see* also Gambling

Gross revenues, 10, 11
Gross wagers, 9, 29, *See* also Handle
Handle, 5, 7
Horse racing, 12-17
    attendance, 16
    handle, 17
    history of, 14-16
    number of, 16
    types of, 16
Indian Gaming Regulatory Act, 10-11
Jackson, Andrew, 2
Jai-alai, 12, 18
Kopel, Rep. Jerry, testimony of 48
Leisure Economy, 8
Lotteries, 2, 28ff
    debate, 41-48
    in history, 2, 28
    prizes, 31-32
    sales, 30-31
    taxes on, 32
    types of, 30
    world, 33
Lotto, 30, *See* also Lotteries
Mississippi River, 2
Progressives, 3
Puncke, Martin M., testimony of, 43
Queen Elizabeth I, 17
Reform Movement, 2, 3
Riverboats, 2, 25-26
Roulette, 2
Smith, Owen Patrick, 17
Sulky race, 16
Thoroughbred, *See* horse racing
Van Buren, Martin, 2
Washington, George, 2
Whicker, Dr. Marcia Lynn, testimony of, 41-43